THE MEANING OF CHRISTIAN BAPTISM

CLEAN!

WILLIAM G. JOHNSSON

Southern Publishing Association, Nashville, Tennessee

Dedication

To Thomas H. Blincoe,
dean, colleague, counselor, friend

Copyright © 1980 by
Southern Publishing Association

This book was
Edited by Richard Coffen
Designed by Dean Tucker

Type set: 10/12 Melior
Printed in U.S.A.

Library of Congress Cataloging in Publication Data

Johnsson, William G   1934-
    Clean! : The meaning of Christian baptism.

    1. Baptism.   I. Title.
BV811.2.J63   234'.161   80-15681
ISBN 0-8127-0293-X

Contents

Preface

Baptism is a Christian practice hallowed by the centuries. Therein lie perils.

On the one hand, some may regard baptism as merely a form, a ritual in which one takes part because "it's the thing to do." Many young people who grow up in the shadow of the church and who are baptized at eleven, twelve, or thirteen years of age probably do so out of peer pressure or the charm of a visiting Week of Prayer speaker.

On the other hand, baptism may remain shrouded in mystery, theological fuzziness, and superstition. Some may think of it as having almost magical powers or heavy overtones of judgment. In either case much is lost: Religious familiarity hatches vampires that suck out the life of the church.

I feel convinced that there is a lack of understanding, and much misunderstanding, about Christian baptism. This book is intended to provide a straightforward, Biblical response to that need. It aims not merely to list the New Testament facts about baptism but to *reflect* on their meaning. For the early Christians, baptism held deep meaning. I hope that *Clean!* might recapture that spirit. I will endeavor to show also that the topic answers to the basic needs of every person, whether ancient or modern.

Clean! speaks to all Christians. I have avoided scholarly

notes and a bibliography. Also I have tried to weed out theological jargon, denominational clichés, and "pat" explanations of baptism in an attempt to present its meaning in terms that modern man can understand.

The book goes out with the prayer that as Christians read it they may better understand their own baptism. Further, that those not yet baptized may see the beauty of this ancient Christian rite and may exclaim with the Ethiopian official: "See, here is water! What is to prevent my being baptized?" (Acts 8:36 *).

---

*Unless otherwise noted, all Bible verses are from the Revised Standard Version:

1

The Quest for Cleansing

For us He would provide a bath
Wherein to cleanse from sin,
And drown the bitterness of death
In His own blood and wounds,
And so create new life.

The eye itself sees but the water
As man pours water forth
But faith in the spirit understands
The power of Jesus Christ's blood.

These words from one of Martin Luther's hymns are typical of Christian hymnody. Over and over, in lines such as Cowper's "There is a fountain filled with blood" or Nicholson's "Now wash me, and I shall be whiter than snow," believers have confessed their state of defilement and their appreciation for the cleansing that Christ's blood supplies.

What many Christians may not realize is that this language belongs in a wider context. In fact, it has counterparts in every religion. It is universal in scope and timeless in its expression of the human condition. Thus baptism, moving within the orbit of defilement and purgation, points to a deep-seated need of mankind.

It will be well for us to look for a while at this universal phenomenon. As we notice how widespread and enduring is the awareness of defilement, and how intense the quest for cleansing, and as we probe the nature of defilement and the purification that mankind so zealously seeks, we shall better grasp the meaning of baptism as cleansing by Christ.

The Universal Sense of Defilement

As the Aztec priest presented the newborn babe for ceremonial bathing he intoned to the Goddess of the Flowing Waters: "Wash him and deliver him from impurities as thou knowest should be, for he is confided to thy power. Cleanse him of the contamination he hath received from his parents; let the water take away the soil and stain, and let him be freed from all taint."

Here is an idea fundamental in the consciousness of the human race. Mankind is defiled and needs cleansing. Over and over the awareness flows up from the subconscious mind to outward expression. It surfaces in a host of manifestations, both of a religious and a secular character.

It is the language of Isaiah who bemoans, " 'Woe is me! For I am lost; for I am a man of unclean lips, and I dwell in the midst of a people of unclean lips; for my eyes have seen the King, the Lord of hosts!' " (6:5). It is the language of the "negative confession" from ancient Egypt: "I have not defiled myself in the pure places of the god of my city." It is the language of the *Book of Revelations* in the modern Japanese religion of Tenrikyo: "When you have swept dust cleanly, I shall certainly bring you a miraculous salvation."

And who could forget the gripping scene from Shakespeare's *Macbeth* as Lady Macbeth descends the stairs in her sleep, incessantly "washing" her hands as she cries:

> Yet here's a spot. . . .
> What, will these hands ne'er be clean? . . .

> Here's the smell of the blood still.
> All the perfumes of Arabia
> will not sweeten this little hand.
> Oh, oh, oh!

Or the words of remorse of her husband, party with her to the gruesome murder of his rivals:

> What hands are here? ha!
>   they pluck out mine eyes.
> Will all great Neptune's ocean
>   wash this blood
> Clean from my hand?
> No, this my hand will rather
> The multitudinous seas incarnadine,
> Making the green one red.

Not only man is defiled. While he is the focus of religious concern, the pollution may extend to places and objects of secular or ritualistic usage. In the Book of Leviticus, for instance, dwellings (14:33ff), garments (13:47ff), and beds (15:4ff) could become defiled. And in the Shinto religion of Japan, time itself becomes defiled and has to be cleansed in an annual ceremony.

The understanding and expression of defilement vary greatly from one religion to another and from one culture to another. Even within a particular religion or culture wide differences occur. What this multiform expression reveals, however, is that defilement is a *human* problem. It is basic, not some quirk or oddity, some flotsam thrown up sporadically by the sea of religions.

Paul Ricoeur in *The Symbolism of Evil* has studied the language of mankind's confessions. He notes that man's chief way of understanding himself is: I am dirty; I am stained; I am defiled. Throughout the course of human change and development the symbol persists.

We see it all around us, even in our modern, secular society. We refer to it in expressions like "dirty money," "dirty politics," "filthy story," "dark deed." The modern cult of the bathroom is more than simply a matter of our knowledge of hygiene, and so is our preoccupation with spring-cleaning, washing machines, dishwashers, and vacuum cleaners. By all these practices and gadgets we perpetuate defilement rituals, though in a desacralized manner.

The Nature of Defilement

The main idea of defilement is that of a physical stain or blot, that is, dirt. So it is to be washed, swept, or rubbed away. In some religions elaborate ceremonies of "sending away" are performed: a boat is cast adrift, carrying with it the "sins" of the tribe; sacrifices are offered to absorb the impurities of the town; or the sins of the community are transferred to bundles of grass.

Yet defilement, while expressed in the concrete symbol of dirt, is always more than an external matter. It points to an inner, spiritual problem. It brings to light man's sense that, in some way, he is out of harmony with the basic order of the cosmos. Defilement tells us that man is not merely concerned or anxious but that there is a *supernatural* factor involved. It implies that man, in some way, is responsible to God for the state in which he finds himself. He is dirty—dirty before a pure God and must give account of himself for it.

Let us probe further into the nature of defilement as revealed by the universal human concern. We note that over and over the "dirt" of defilement is viewed as a contagion. The reformer Zwingli, for instance, described sin as a "sickness." The Parsis of India—survivors of the ancient faith of Zoroaster—provide an even more dramatic example. They, along with many other cultures, view a corpse as an agent of extreme defilement. The corpse can neither be burned nor buried, lest it defile fire or earth. Hence it is exposed to the elements and the vultures in "towers of silence."

So defilement is more than a problem of individual concern. The polluted person is a polluter—he spreads his contagion throughout his community and defiles the sacred places. Thus, we read this injunction from the people of the Qumran community: "No man shall lie with a woman in the city of the Sanctuary, to defile the city of the Sanctuary with their uncleanness."

In many religions, therefore, the defiled person comes under severe strictures. He is banished from worship. He is separated from his fellows. In extreme cases, he may even face execution. In a sense, defilement has made him or her less than a full human being, and so the person is cut off from the life of society and cut off from deity.

Three words point to the specifically *religious* character of defilement—power, death, and order.

First, defilement is negative power. This is why it is dangerous. It is conceived of in much the same way as we think of disease. Most of us have not actually *seen* bacteria or viruses. They exist for us as quasi-material substances manifested by their functional power to be transmitted and to cause ill effects.

Second, defilement shows us the plight of man as he confronts death and the fear of death. As we noticed above, in many religions a corpse is thought of as the most unclean object, that is, it is laden with negative power. Likewise, bodily issues and functions are intimately associated with defilement. Thus, it seems likely that man's religious concern with defilement is inextricably bound up with his desire to promote and prolong life and to avoid death. Defilement is the power of death.

Third, dirt indicates disorder. It is an offense to the

organizing character of mind. Likewise death is an
anomaly. It marks a breach in society, a disordering of
communal organization. Dirt and death are of a kind. They
represent that which is out of place, disrupting the order of
society and ultimately of the cosmos.

Defilement, then, is a quasi-material, quasi-moral, evil
power that is readily transmittable. It represents the force
of disorder and chaos that stands over against the individual's existence, his society, and finally the cosmos.

Purification

Purification is the counterpart of defilement. As there is
a widespread, continuing sense of defilement, so there is a
restlessness within the consciousness of defilement and a
studied endeavor to break loose.

Over and over this longing comes to expression. "Purity is best for man from his birth," said Zarathustra. "Mary,
God has chosen and purified thee," said the angel to Mary
in the Koran. And this ancient hymn from the Avesta,
scripture for the Zoroastrians, states:

> "We sacrifice to the undying, shining,
> swift-horsed Sun. . . .
> "And when the sun rises up, then the earth,
> made by Ahura, becomes clean; the running wa-
> ters become clean, the waters of the wells be-
> come clean, the waters of the sea become clean,
> the standing waters become clean, all the holy
> creatures, the creatures of the Good Spirit, be-
> come clean."

As defilement is first viewed as dirt, dust, spot, or stain,
so purgation in its fundamental symbols stands for a washing away, a wiping off, a making clean. As defilement is

manifested as infectious, negative power, so purification appears as health—the vigor of wholesome potency. As there are degrees of defilement, so there are degrees of purification. And as defilement is interiorized, so purgation moves from rites dealing with the external body to the purifying of the inner life. But just as the primary symbol of defilement as dirt, disorder, and anomaly is never lost even though an internalization has taken place, so the symbol of purification retains its essential moment of cleansing, ordering, making whole.

Purification points to man's state of pristine purity. It sees defilement as an intrusion into the cosmos, and it longs to return to paradise. Defilement stands for what man *is*. Purgation for what he may *become*.

If defilement is negative power, purification is a state of positive power. Just as defilement carries the aura of death, so purification throbs with life. Pollution is a state of disorder. Cleansing is a restoration of status from the separated to the integrated, the profane to the holy, the disordered to the ordered, from anxiety to joy and peace.

Thus purification is a transition, an initiation. It is a regeneration, a rebirth that opens the doors of religious privilege. And it is a healing that removes the contagion of defilement and unifies the individual, the society, or the cosmos to a state of order and continuity.

Agents of Purification

The means of purification are legion. Among them, water is the universally efficacious medium. Pure, clean water is called for. It is often termed a "fountain" or "living" water.

India and Japan perpetuate the concern with purgation on a large scale. In both we see the preeminent place of water as the medium of purification.

Rivers have a peculiar significance for the Hindus. I

have met bands of pilgrims on the Indian road. In the high fastnesses of the Himalayas or on the paved way outside the large city, one quickly recognizes them—not so much by their saffron robes or bundles of belongings slung on the back as by their sense of purpose, of religious devotion. How far have they come? Perhaps hundreds of miles. Where are they going? No matter what the place, you may be certain of one thing: they will take a sacred bath there. The climax of the trek will come as the weary members of the band plunge into the snow-fed waters of Kedrinath or Badrinath or into the warm waters of Benares or Nasik.

In Japan's native religion, Shinto, the essential element likewise is the cold bath. To be complete, bathing should take place in turn at the mouth of a river, near the source of a river, in the sea, under a waterfall, and in a spring or well—all in a state of complete nudity.

Although water is a universal agent of purification, it is not the sole medium or necessarily the most potent. Indeed, the symbol of blood intrudes itself as an agent of superlative power. Among the Aztecs, for example, every purification ceremony involved the use of blood. It was "the precious liquid." And notice again William Cowper's hymn:

> There is a fountain filled with blood,
> Drawn from Immanuel's veins;
> And sinners plunged beneath that flood,
> Lose all their guilty stains.

Here the prime figure is water baptism, as shown by the terms *fountain* and *plunged*. Yet the water has been transformed into blood, even the blood of Christ. This alone can purge defilement and impart new life.

Many other agents of purification might be listed. Just as seemingly any object may be a source of defilement, so almost any object may lend itself for purgation. Most widespread, however, are the following: beating, fire, smoke, and salt.

Several practices apart from these are clearly directed toward the purification of the body. Such are fasting, celibacy, and pilgrimage. For example, in Islam, a pilgrimage well performed is supposed to purify a person from all his sins so that he becomes as sinless as when he was born.

Some religious observances, however, are wholly concerned with "internal" purification. Prayer, meditation, concentration, control of the thoughts and emotions, and confession are examples. Buddhism in its various forms emphasizes this type of purgation.

Yet purification is always of the *whole* person, regardless of the means. Just as defilement is never viewed as wholly physical or wholly "spiritual," so the cleansing sought so assiduously by the religious devotee embraces the entire being.

The Endless Cycle

Only as we view defilement and cleansing from a religious perspective will we gain a correct view of their nature and interrelations. Defilement taboos and purification rites must be approached not primarily from the viewpoint of public health. Certain benefits in the area of hygiene and medical practice may have ensued from some of them, but such benefits were merely incidental and derivative—just as the man who goes to church may enjoy physical relaxation.

Defilement and purification point to a fundamental aspect of the human self-awareness. When a person feels "I am dirty" and seeks to be made clean, he is trying to express his relation to deity, his understanding of his place in the cosmos, and his confrontation of his finitude in the face of death. So, while many laws and rites that deal with pollution and its removal seem wooden and formal, devoid of moral or spiritual worth, in fact they tell us much about humanity. They expose to us mankind stripped of pride, in radical unease before deity and cosmos, and striving to attain to peace with both.

The following transition lies at the foundation of this religious thought-world:

Defilement ⟶ Purgation

Here are two states, one the mirror-image of the other. Whereas defilement comes to expression as a quasi-material, quasi-moral, infectious state accompanied by feelings of dread, loss, and separation, so purgation is a quasi-material, quasi-moral state of wholeness and blessing.

Yet the correspondence is not absolute. Defilement is the state of the *is*, purgation that of the *ought-to-be*. The present continually hammers home the disparity: Everyone continually is defiled instead of being what he ought to be. Defilement looms large as the "problem" that ever confronts mankind and arises to dash our efforts to rest in the state of purgation. In other words, the balance tilts toward defilement:

Defilement ⟶ Purgation

Another way of expressing the idea is:

Defilement ⟶ Purgation

Here is a picture of man as *homo religiosus*—man the religious. He is constantly aware of his falling short of what he might be, of what he ought to be. He is dirty, defiled, and responsible for it. He seeks ways and means to achieve the wholeness that cleansing brings, and he finds temporary relief from defilement. But only temporary! The contagion of pollution soon reinfects him, dirties his state, and pulls him back to where he began, He is caught up in an endless cycle of defilement—purification—redefilement.

Defilement and purification sound a distinctly somber note. The accent falls again and again on what has been lost, what might be, how far short mankind is from the primal state of purity. While purification provides an upbeat approach to existence, the consciousness of its unattainability as a permanent state transposes the song of life into a minor key.

We may now summarize our sketch of mankind's quest for cleansing. On one side we see painted in vivid colors man as he is—dirty, alone, despairing. Defilement is a state of semideath, of disorder for the individual and for the cosmos. On the other we see the religious vision, the state of cleansing. Here there is bliss, harmony, order, integration, power, life, and fellowship with God. But that state is elusive. It may (so it is hoped) be attained through some purifying agent or ritual, but it cannot be held. The infection of defilement will wrest control again.

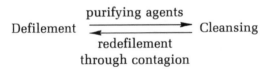

We have deliberately refrained from using New Testament examples in the above description. Many examples doubtless will have come to the mind of the thoughtful reader. Our concern has been to provide the backdrop for our study of the meaning of baptism as the New Testament sets it out.

Already we have seen that there is a massive weight of

evidence outside the Bible. Over and over man has expressed his feelings of uneasiness in terms of defilement and has sought for cleansing by various means. This evidence both precedes and follows New Testament times, and it grows daily—even secular society shows it up in desacralized forms.

Obviously we must take account of this universal expression of man's religious needs. The discussion of Christian baptism can be intelligent only as we see the practice in the light of these widespread, enduring phenomena. And further—we may better grasp its own meaning as we are aware of what is "going on" outside Christianity.

Let no one fear that such an approach will paganize or water down the distinctiveness of baptism. Indeed, it is as we see the common elements that we can be ready to grasp the uniqueness of Christian baptism. It is against the backdrop of man's universal quest for cleansing that we must embark upon our study of the New Testament answer and solution.

So we turn to the New Testament itself. As we seek to probe its data carefully and reflectively, we shall refrain from drawing parallels with the data of this chapter. When we have completed our study of the material and pause for a final, bird's-eye view of our topic (chapter 7), we shall draw some lines of comparison and contrast. But our study so far has prepared us, I hope, to approach the New Testament material for what it is—religious, first of all.

Now we are ready to look at the first man to baptize in the New Testament account. What did John the Baptist's rite signify?

2

The Baptist
—Cleansing Announced

John the Baptist appears with dramatic suddenness in the Gospel stories. For several centuries the prophetic impulse of Israel had ceased. Now it revived in a brilliant upsurge. The man from the desert—alone, aloof, crystal clear in understanding of his mission, and fearless in its proclamation—stood in the line of Jeremiah and Amos, Isaiah and Elijah.

No wonder he created a stir! His very appearance and mode of life recalled Elijah of old and called into question the canons of respectability. More than these, however, his words—direct, uncompromising, urgent—demanded attention. So the crowds flocked to the desert to see and hear for themselves. Common folk, soldiers, scribes, Levites, and Pharisees all felt the pull of the prophetic message. A particular rite accompanied John's words. He baptized. All four Gospels mention this activity, and Mark's calls him "the baptizer" (1:4). So common is the idea of baptism to us that John's significance likely escapes us. The point is this: *Christian baptism has its origin in the work of John the Baptist, not in Jesus.* The New Testament, which throughout presupposes baptism as integral to the Christian religion, nowhere derives the practice from the Lord Himself. While the person and death of Jesus invest the rite with added meaning, its roots reach back to the prophet of the desert.

The Greek word used for baptism, *baptisma,* demonstrates this fact. *Baptisma* occurs a total of twenty times in the New Testament. Thirteen times it refers to the baptism by John, four times to Christian baptism, and three times it is a metaphor of Jesus' death. But the word itself was a newcomer to human vocabulary. It was not found at all in secular or sacred writings before the New Testament. Like the Baptist himself, it suddenly appeared on the stage of human history. Baptism, then, *characterized* the ministry of John and *originated* with him.

Obviously we must give close attention to John's rite. If Christian baptism has its roots there, what was its primal meaning? Why, for instance, did John call on people to manifest their repentance *by being baptized*—something that the prophets before him had never suggested? And what of the relationship of Jesus to John? Why was Jesus Himself baptized by John?

Let us trace through these issues carefully. A clear concept of baptism in its origins will put us on the right track for grasping its Christian meaning. First, however, we should try to understand John in the light of his times. We saw above that the word *baptism* is unique to the New Testament. But did not the Jews already practice ritual washings? Wherein did the *baptisma* proclaimed and administered by John differ from them?

Jewish Antecedents to Baptism

The Old Testament contains frequent references to religious washings. For the ceremony of cleansing from leprosy (Leviticus 14:1-9); for purification of men or women after bodily discharges (Leviticus 15); for removal of defilement due to contact with unclean beasts (Leviticus 11:24, 28, 40), with a corpse (Numbers 19:11-13), or with the ashes of the red heifer (Numbers 19:1-10); as well as for the consecration of the Levites (Numbers 8:7, 21), bathing in water was commanded in the law.

As we look at these Old Testament antecedents to baptism, we notice that the Septuagint uses the verb *baptizō* once—the same word used throughout the New Testament for the act of baptizing. We find it as Naaman washed seven times in the Jordan (2 Kings 5:14). In this Old Testament reference *baptizō* must signify "to wash" or "to bathe." In Leviticus 11:32 a similar verb appears—*baptō*. However, the noun *baptisma*, which denotes the act itself, is not employed anywhere before the New Testament.

These facts help us probe the meaning of John's baptism. On the one hand, the fact that the verbs *baptizō* and *baptō* had already been used for religious washings in the Old Testament suggests that to some degree the basic idea of "washing" or "purification" must carry over. When John said, "I baptize you with water," his hearers could not help but think of the Levitical regulations and the story of Naaman. On the other hand, the fact that the noun *baptisma* first occurs in the New Testament suggests that there was an element of *newness*, a going beyond the Jewish ceremonies while retaining a link with them.

Apart from these Old Testament antecedents, we should take note of John's contemporaries. Two groups among the people of John's day were especially concerned with religious washing—the Qumran community and the Jewish proselytes.

The precise number and type of religious lustrations among the people at Qumran is not clear. It is evident, however, that washings in water played an important part in the life of individuals and community. The people by the Dead Sea thought of themselves as a select group, the pure remnant of Israel. Entry into the sect was not easy. Examination, lots, and a probationary period were demanded. A ritual cleansing marked the close of the initial year of probation. After full membership in the sect had been attained, lustrations were frequent, possibly in preparation for the communal sacred meal.

An interesting feature of the Qumran washings was their association with the idea of judgment. The Dead Sea people looked for the imminent Day of the Lord, when Yahweh would visit Jerusalem and its corrupt priesthood with punishment and the people from Qumran would emerge from the Dead Sea wilderness to take over the land. They even appealed to the prophecy of Isaiah 40:3—the voice crying in the wilderness—as its fulfillment. Thus, to enter into the religious washing of Qumran was to identify oneself with a separated community, one that was poised for divine intervention and messianic activity.

There are some close similarities with John the Baptist and his message here. We shall come back to the Qumran sect later in this chapter. After we have analyzed the preaching and work of the Baptist, we shall better be able to see the points of contact and difference.

The first century AD was also a period of considerable Jewish missionary activity. Jesus Himself referred to the zeal of Israel's leaders to make proselytes (Matthew 23:15). The convert to Judaism underwent two religious rites— circumcision and washing. We know of these regulations because of controversy among the rabbis as to the relative importance of each. Whereas at first only circumcision was expected of the proselyte, the conversion of Arabs and Samaritans who already had been circumcised as well as the large number of non-Jewish women converts led to the addition of proselyte washing.

We cannot be sure of all the details of proselyte lustration. It apparently was self-administered, involved a total immersion of the body, and was connected with repentance.

Nor do we know how early the practice arose. The first clear attestation of it is about AD 80, half a century after John began to preach and baptize. It is possible that the rite arose out of the impact of Christianity on Judaism. It is not likely, however, that the Jews would adopt a Christian practice. Rather, the practice was probably already established when John began to preach a "baptism of repentance"—a natural extension of the Old Testament regulations concerning purification.

Did John, then, borrow the idea of baptism from Jewish proselyting? Once again we must hold the question until we have studied carefully John's own teaching and practice. Only after we have compared and contrasted the baptism of John with Jewish proselyte lustrations will we be ready to see if *borrowing* is the correct term to use.

The Message of John the Baptist

Five words sum up the preaching of the Baptist as it has come down to us in the Gospel accounts: *repent, kingdom, judgment, ethics, witness.*

The Gospel of Matthew summarizes John's message as: "Repent, for the kingdom of heaven is at hand" (Matthew 3:2). Mark and Luke do not recall these precise words, but they agree that John came "preaching a baptism of repentance for the forgiveness of sins" (Mark 1:4; Luke 3:3).

Repent! The word signifies a change of heart, a reorientation of thinking, a turning around. It is not merely a reconsideration, a change of mind common to all of us in the light of new evidence. No. Repentance is, as it was for John, "for the forgiveness of *sins*." The repentant one is intensely aware of the weight of his sins, of his accountability to a holy God, and of how far short he comes. Instead of a life directed toward the ways of sin, he "comes to himself," like the prodigal son, and turns back to a loving Father's home. In the words of Ellen G. White, "Repentance includes sorrow for sin and a turning away from it" (*Steps to Christ*, p. 23).

Sounding the call to repent, John the Baptist stood squarely in the line of Israel's prophets. Over and over they called upon Israel to turn again, to return to Yahweh. But the direction of John's message was different. Whereas the Old Testament messengers addressed the nation at large, the Baptist spoke to the individual. While many indeed responded (Mark 1:4, 5), the confession was personal.

Further, John's call was not a mere reiteration of the nation's apostasy from God and a heart cry for it to repent. His challenge was: "Repent, *for the kingdom of heaven is at hand.*" That is, not just repentance because of a breaking of the covenant with Yahweh, but turning to God because of what He was about to do. With the "kingdom" idea John's preaching came in the context of warning, imminence, urgency.

His hearers were familiar with the phrase. He did not need to explain to them that "the kingdom" signified divine intervention, the breaking in of the Eternal into the world order. Already the Old Testament had laid the groundwork for such thinking. As the centuries went by, and especially after the Jews had lost their king and their independence, expectation and wistful longing looked for the God of the covenant to act again in dramatic fashion for the deliverance of His people. As the blowing of trumpets anciently sounded the note to get ready for the Day of Atonement, so John called upon the people to prepare themselves for God's new act.

What thoughts must have stirred the hearts of the people as they heard John proclaim the soon arrival of the kingdom! For many there would have arisen an upsurge of nationalistic fervor, a longing to see the hated Roman troops of the occupation driven out. But his message had a different cut. It announced judgment on *mankind,* not on just the enemy. "Who warned you to flee from the wrath to come?" he challenged the Pharisees and Sadducees. "Even now the axe is laid to the root of the trees; every tree therefore that does not bear good fruit is cut down and thrown into the fire. . . . His winnowing fork is in his hand, and he will clear his threshing floor and gather his wheat into the granary, but the chaff he will burn with unquenchable fire" (Matthew 3:7, 10-12).

John called for a way of life that would correspond with the times—the times of the judgment of the kingdom. Repentance did not involve a temporary return to God in order that one might be ready for the divine intervention. Rather, it was to profoundly affect behavior, or *ethics.* "Bear fruit that befits repentance" (Matthew 3:8), was his challenge. He warned against a smug reliance on ancestry. "Do not presume to say to yourselves, 'We have Abraham as our father'; for I tell you, God is able from these stones to raise up children to Abraham" (Matthew 3:9). Instead, repentance was to filter down to the nitty-gritty of life, coloring every relationship. It would make the repentant one generous and kind. It would enable the tax collectors to be fair in their work. It would turn every soldier away from violence and oppression (Luke 3:10-14).

Finally, John's preaching involved *witness.* His announcement of the coming kingdom of heaven and the impending revelation of God's judgment on the sinfulness of mankind was attached to a person, One who was mightier, whose sandals he was not worthy to carry (Matthew 3:11). That One would baptize them "with the Holy Spirit and with fire" (Luke 3:16).

The Gospel of John specifically designates the Baptist as witness. Indeed, his entire role is subsumed under this idea: "There was a man sent from God, whose name was John. He came for testimony, to bear witness to the light, that all might believe through him. He was not the light, but came to bear witness to the light" (John 1:6-8). John 1:19-34 shows John fulfilling this role as he denied his own importance and directed his hearers to the Son of God, God's Word incarnate: "And I have seen and have borne witness that this is the Son of God" (John 1:34).

Repentance, kingdom, judgment, ethics, witness—this was the message of John the Baptist. It was a clarion call for a radical change of thinking and living in view of the impending kingdom of heaven with its One who was far greater than the Baptist himself.

The Meaning of John's Baptism

John's work differed in two respects from that of the prophets of old. As we saw above, his call for repentance was tied to a time frame. It was repentance in view of the impending intervention of God—an intervention that would go beyond all previous divine acts on behalf of mankind. Second, his call for repentance was tied to a public *act*. Apart from the reorientation of thinking, the return to God and ethical living, repentance was to be demonstrated by submission to the rite of baptism. His was "a baptism of repentance for the forgiveness of sins."

These two distinguishing marks of John's work converge in a single idea—the *eschatological* factor. That is, the time, the time of the coming of the kingdom of God, demanded an *extraordinary* type of repentance. It was a repentance that would put itself on display by a public act.

The Scriptures tell us that all sorts of people came out to hear John and were baptized. Tax gatherers, common folk, soldiers—John baptized them in the Jordan. (The Pharisees and Sadducees also came out, but they refused to submit to the call for baptism!) What did their baptism mean to these people?

At the very least, baptism indicated their belief in the trustworthiness of John and his message. All the common people were "convinced that John was a prophet" (Luke 20:6), a late flowering of that line from the glorious history of Israel. By submitting to his baptism they put the stamp of their approval on his work.

Further, baptism indicated that they were *serious* about the need for repentance. John's "altar call" was not as easy as those of past preachers. Possibly the person coming forward for baptism exposed himself to the risk of ridicule from his friends. After all, no previous prophet had ever called for such a lustration. Nowhere did the law demand it. But the ringing words of the desert preacher had pierced home: The sincere desire for repentance would be publically demonstrated as he had proclaimed.

Third, the Old Testament associations of religious washings must have been aroused. As Israel from ancient times had acknowledged the holiness of her God and her own defilement in view of that absolute purity by religious lustrations, so the person coming to John for baptism was confessing: "I am dirty. I turn from my uncleanness to the purity of Yahweh. I need to be washed clean in His sight!"

The eschatological factor, however, must receive emphasis. By baptism the candidate demonstrated to Israel at large that he believed *the time was at hand*—the time for "the kingdom" with its judgment and One mightier than John. An extraordinary moment in history demanded an extraordinary religious response. That response was baptism.

There may have been yet another aspect to the meaning of John's baptism. Because the evidence is fragmentary, the conclusion must be tentative, but it is likely that a community significance was involved. In other words, baptism was the point of entry into the group who shared the eschatological hope and repentance. We do know that John had disciples (Matthew 9:14; Mark 2:18; Luke 7:18ff; John 1:35; 3:25; 4:1). We also know that long after his death there was at least one group whose identity stemmed from his baptism (Acts 19:1-3). In fact, a Mesopotamian sect, the Mandaeans, to this day continues to revere John the Baptist and to give him pride of place over Jesus. Because John's work was so short and so quickly overshadowed by Jesus', however, the community of John's baptism—if it ever existed—was short-lived. We have no evidence that John's preaching called for such community-building.

We are now prepared to take another look at the lustrations at Qumran and the Jewish baptism of proselytes. Our study of John's message and the meaning of his baptism has highlighted the uniqueness of his rite, despite some similarities to practices of his religious contemporaries.

The washings at Qumran were part of a rigidly sectarian way of thought and life. It was the little group by the Dead Sea who were Yahweh's chosen ones—the world at large was doomed for His wrath. John, however, lacked this note of religious exclusivism. His call was implicitly universalistic. Nor did he call for a long period of preparation for candidates. The attitude of the heart (which would be manifested by conduct) was the essence of the word *repentance*. More significantly, John's baptism was a one-time affair, while the washings at Qumran were repeated.

It is true that both the Baptist and the convenanters at Qumran were not part of the Jerusalem establishment and that they both had a strong eschatological emphasis. The messianic expectation was quite different in each case, however. While the ascetics at Qumran looked for their triumph in the return to Jerusalem, the Coming One of John's preaching and baptism would arrive with the fan and fire of judgment. In fine, John's rite was associated with a *warning* to all; Qumran's with an attitude of inward-looking scrupulosity. Or, we may say, John *bap-*

tized, the Qumranites practiced lustrations.

The so-called proselyte baptism is even further removed. The rite itself was self-administered. It was not associated with divine pardon. The eschatological factor—judgment, kingdom, the Coming One—was altogether lacking. And the most important difference: John's baptism was for *all*, but only non-Jews could be proselytes! The religious washing of the convert to Judaism rather belongs within the context of those numerous Old Testament ablutions. Like them, it pointed to an act of purification, simply and wholly.

So it is not strange that *baptisma*, the New Testament noun for baptism, does not occur in the Greek Old Testament or in any other writings before the New Testament. We may feel safe to conclude that John's baptism was a newcomer among the religious acts of mankind. Its meaning was original and unique to the message of the preacher in the desert.

One last issue remains: Why did Jesus submit to John's baptism? What was its meaning for Him?

John and Jesus

That Jesus was baptized by John must have embarrassed some of the early Christians. The rivalry felt by some of John's disciples toward the growing movement of Jesus (John 3:26-30) would have exacerbated the problem. Yet the Gospel writers frankly acknowledge Jesus' baptism, without any attempt at concealment. Further, they record that Jesus Himself made appeal to John's testimony about Him (John 5:33-36) as well as to John's authority (Luke 20:4; Matthew 21:25; Mark 11:30). And He publicly praised John in words of the highest commendation (Matthew 11:7-11; Luke 7:24-28).

But Jesus was no disciple of John. His coming forward

at the Jordan did not signify that He desired to be attached to John as a follower. Nowhere is there any hint of such a relationship, even for a short time. Indeed, the Gospel of Matthew points in the opposite direction. It tells us that John was reluctant to baptize Jesus: "I need to be baptized by you, and do you come to me?" (Matthew 3:14).

John's statement also corrects the possible embarrassment of Jesus' baptism. It shows us that the key element of repentance was not involved. Jesus was *not* baptized to demonstrate His turning to God in the light of the dawning kingdom of heaven.

Then why did He request baptism? We are not told clearly. We have only the cryptic reply with which He overrode John's objections to baptizing Him: "Let it be so now; for thus it is fitting for us to fulfil all righteousness" (verse 15). Let us try to probe the meaning of those terse words: "to fulfil all righteousness."

First, by His own baptism Jesus put His stamp of approval on both the mission of John and the rite of baptism that was its hallmark. He showed that He believed John to be a genuine prophet and His work to be of God. That is, Jesus *identified Himself* with the movement of John.

Second, Jesus' baptism had a deep personal significance. This was not in terms of the quest for inner cleansing but of His own unique mission. In all four Gospels the commencement of the ministry of Jesus is associated with His meeting with the Baptist (Matthew 3:13-17; Mark 1:9-12; Luke 3:21, 22; John 1:29-51). His coming to the Baptist at the Jordan showed His answer to His own call to mission. Perhaps that is why, when He approached the climax of that mission as He made His last journey toward Jerusalem, He spoke again of baptism, the baptism of His death: "I have a baptism to be baptized with; and how I am constrained until it is accomplished!" (Luke 12:50).

Yet there is more to the idea of fulfilling all righteousness. "All righteousness" points us back to the "law and to the prophets"—the entire Old Testament. We hear again parallel words of the Lord during the course of His ministry: "Think not that I have come to abolish the law and the prophets; I have come not to abolish them but to fulfil them" (Matthew 5:17). "So whatever you wish that men would do to you, do so to them; for this is the law and the prophets" (Matthew 7:12). "On these two commandments depend all the law and the prophets" (Matthew 22:40). And *fulfill* throughout the Gospel of Matthew is associated with *deed*, with something that happens which concretizes the Old Testament predictions and expectation (1:22; 2:15, 17, 23; 4:14; 8:17; 12:17; 13:35; 21:4; 26:54; 27:9). Thus, by His baptism, Jesus converged the entire Old Testament upon Himself. In Himself He was the concretization of its hopes and its meaning. By word and by deed He brought it to realization. His baptism signified that the age of "the kingdom" had arrived at last, that age to which all before had been moving.

Can we take one more step in the search for understanding? The doing of God's will, which is the essence of fulfilling all righteousness, was more than the commencement of mission, more than the inauguration of the age of the kingdom of heaven. By coming forward to be baptized, Jesus identified Himself with the sinner in His need of God's righteousness. This first public act set the stage for the service that He would give to mankind. Over and over He went to the people, wherever there was need, wherever there was an aching heart or an aching body, whenever there was a spirit hungering and thirsting for God. He would take upon Himself the woes and sicknesses of mankind (Matthew 8:17), and at last He would bear their sins to a cross.

So the baptism of Jesus was unlike any other's. It was an act of affirmation (of John's movement), of commitment (to

His own mission), of identification (with the frailty of humanity). Thus it fulfilled all righteousness.

Now we can see more clearly the relationship between the work of the Baptist and of Jesus. John stood, as it were, at the hinge of the ages. The old age of "the law and the prophets" was about to come to an end. It would be gathered up in the new age that would bring to fulfillment the hopes, anticipations, longings, and expectations of the old—the age of the kingdom. John was the herald of the new age: He announced that its dawn was about to break. With the commencement of Jesus' mission, the dawn broke.

The Gospels bring out John's pivotal role by way of two complementary passages. When Mark commences to write, he directs us to "the beginning of the gospel of Jesus Christ, the Son of God" but leads with the work of John the Baptist (Mark 1:1-8). For Mark, the beginning of the Good News of the kingdom is inseparable from the work of the Baptist. In Luke, however, we read: "The law and the prophets were until John; since then the good news of the kingdom of God is preached, and every one enters it violently" (Luke 16:16; see also Matthew 11:11, 12). Here the preaching of John is placed within the context of the old age. Only after it do people enter the kingdom of God.

What, then, of John's baptism—did it belong to the old age? Can we say that baptism has passed away for Christians?

That would be strange reasoning indeed. As we have seen, baptism was not a part of the law and the prophets. It was a new rite, unique to John. (And even if it had been part of the law and the prophets, the fulfilling of them certainly did not mean their abrogation (Matthew 5:17-19; Luke 16:16, 17). John's baptism was an act signifying repentance *in view of the imminent dawn of the new age.* Further, the entering of Jesus Himself upon this rite gave it a significance that should remove all doubts: We may say that *His* baptism puts it squarely in the new age as well. Baptism overlaps the two ages. It commences at the last strokes of the old but flows on in the new.

In the new age, of course, there will be a modification of meaning. Since John's baptism looked forward to the kingdom (whereas that kingdom commenced in the person and work of Jesus) and since John's baptism was entered into in the expectation of the Coming One (whereas Jesus was that One), Christian baptism cannot have exactly the same meaning. Since baptism overlaps the ages, there will be continuities of meaning, but for Christians there will be a dimension of newness.

In the remaining chapters of this book we will explore the meaning of Christian baptism. As we see the richness of ideas associated with this rite, we shall understand how this act, unique to John and retaining some of its primal significance, has gone beyond to develop its own character—one that reflects the person and work of Jesus Christ.

3

Christian Baptism
—Cleansing Through Confession

The eighth chapter of the Book of Acts narrates the encounter between deacon Philip and the Ethiopian official. Led by the Spirit, Philip joined the Ethiopian in his chariot and proceeded to explain how the prophecy of Isaiah 53 was fulfilled in Jesus. As they traveled south along the road to Gaza they came to some water, whereupon the eunuch exclaimed: "See, here is water! What is to prevent my being baptized?" (Acts 8:36). The Bible study of Philip had been effective. Clearly he had mentioned baptism.

An interesting variation occurs in the text at this point. Readers who follow the story in modern translations will notice that the account jumps from verse 36 to verse 38. There is no verse 37. Whereas the ancient manuscripts of Acts have the full story of the Ethiopian's question and his subsequent baptism by Philip, most omit the official's words recorded as verse 37 in the King James Version: "And Philip said, If thou believest with all thine heart, thou mayest. And he answered and said, I believe that Jesus Christ is the Son of God."

If these words are not original, how did they ever find a place in Acts? We do not know for certain, but most likely the official's purported words were a standard baptismal confession from the early centuries of Christianity. Some overzealous scribe, believing, perhaps, that the Christian practices of his day must have been followed in the time of the apostles, took the liberty to put the standard declaration of the baptismal candidate on the lips of the Ethiopian.

These remarks prepare us for the first major idea about Christian baptism: *It involves confession.* By *confession* we intend more than the acknowledgment of one's sins to a priest or in private before God. Rather, confession signifies a public statement, a profession. The New Testament, for example, uses it fairly frequently in this sense. "Therefore, holy brethren, who share in a heavenly call, consider Jesus, the apostle and high priest of our confession" (Hebrews 3:1). "And every tongue [should] confess that Jesus Christ is Lord, to the glory of God the Father" (Philippians 2:11). "Whoever confesses that Jesus is the Son of God, God abides in him, and he in God" (1 John 4:15).

Although the words of Acts 8:37 are probably not original, they reflect the thinking of the early Christians about the need for open acknowledgment to accompany baptism. That is, word and deed are linked. The public declaration is followed by a public act.

Let us explore the nature of this "confessional" aspect of baptism. We shall see that it has two aspects—the acknowledgment of the person of Jesus as the Christ (the Christological confession) and the confession of one's identification with Jesus in His death (the solidarity confession). Then we shall be ready to consider the implications of these ideas for Christian life and baptismal practice.

The Christological Confession

As the convert to Christianity stood by the baptismal waters, he confessed to the assembled onlookers his faith in Jesus as the Christ. The earliest declaration was probably, "I believe that Jesus is Lord." This is why Paul wrote in

Romans 10:9: "If you confess with your lips that Jesus is Lord and believe in your heart that God raised him from the dead, you will be saved." Later, as we have seen, the confession was changed to: "I believe that Jesus Christ is the Son of God."

What was involved in such a confession of Jesus, by spoken word and confirming act?

It signified, first, the renunciation of all other "lords." The ancient world abounded in them. There were the time-honored deities of Greece and Rome—Zeus—or Jupiter—Mars, Athena, Apollo, Aphrodite, and so on. And there were new gods and goddesses that had infiltrated the empire from the East—Isis and Osiris from Egypt, the Great Mother from Phrygia, Mithras from Persia. These new religions—the "mysteries"—were colorful and emotional and held out personal fellowship with the deity by way of initiations and secret ceremonies. And there were also the ancestral gods of the Romans, the tutelary deities of hearth and door and of field and crop, for every aspect of life.

But Christians had renounced all such claims to worship. In a world of pluralistic and competing religious allegiances, they acknowledged but one Lord—Jesus Christ. Throughout the New Testament, whenever Christians employed the word lord, they referred to Jesus and Him alone.

Lord—how lightly the word comes to our lips today! We use it in hymns, prayers, and conversation, very often without any thought of the currents of history that swirl around it. Christianity in these days, especially if we live in the West, does not impose the radical physical and social demands upon its followers that it did in the first century AD.

But before the first century closed, it became dangerous to insist on the exclusiveness of Jesus as Lord. The emperor Domitian went beyond all his predecessors. He not only claimed allegiance from his subjects because he was the political head of the empire, but he also called for their veneration because he was god in the flesh! This was the most hideous combination of church and state imaginable. The refusal to call Caesar lord signified disloyalty to the Roman state. It was out of this matrix of ideas that the waves of Roman persecution of Christians originated and continued for another two centuries.

We see, then, the Christ-centeredness of Christian baptism. Just as the baptism of John pointed to hope and belief in the Coming One, so the Christian rite centers in that One. It proclaims to believers and nonbelievers alike that the candidate believes and accepts Jesus of Nazareth as Christ and Lord. The baptismal candidate renounces all other claims to lordship over the life and looks to Jesus as the only hope of salvation.

We cannot overestimate the place of the Christological confession in the Christian religion. In a manner unique among the religions of mankind the Christian faith centers *in a man*—in His person and work, rather than in His teachings, great as they are. This Man, this Carpenter from an obscure village in antiquity, challenges mankind today as He challenged His contemporaries: "Who do you say that I am?" (Matthew 16:15). He calls, as He has always called, to a decision *about Himself*. The question cannot be evaded. The world is called to answer. What was He? A madman? A deceiver? A crook? We cannot avoid His piercing eye. We must make some sort of confession. Reject Him we may—reject His claims about Himself, His relation to God, and His role in the salvation of mankind—but we can never be quite the same again.

And there are those who believe His claims. They are won over by the sheer force of truth and beauty in a human life and death. To them He is love incarnated, nothing less than God in the flesh. So gladly they confess Him as Lord.

Gladly they renounce all other claimants to lordship, hand-
ing over to Him alone the key ring of their lives. Without
having seen Him, they love Him. Though they do not now
see Him, they believe in Him and "rejoice with unutterable
and exalted joy" (1 Peter 1:8). They trust Him, holding in a
crooked world, where every man has his price, that He is
the Faithful One, the one Man worthy of our total commitment.

That confession is made concrete by the act of baptism.
From the beginning, Christians have publicly "confessed"
by this means. The act is, as we have seen, in harmony with
and an extension of the baptism of John. Yet it goes far
beyond John's baptism. Whereas the Coming One was but
one feature of his rite, the person of Jesus *dominates* Christian baptism. The act is a public declaration of His lordship
over the candidate.

But to confess Jesus as Lord means to become a disciple.
We have already seen how the word *lord* is a term of special
Christian import, how it is used by them exclusively for
Jesus. Thus, baptism is the door to discipleship.

Christian baptism, then, concentrates our gaze squarely
on the person of Jesus Christ. It is a *Christological* confession. Yet it is more. It also points to a particular self-
understanding of the candidate, a confession of his identification with Jesus in His death.

The Solidarity Confession

The crowd in Jerusalem for the Feast of Pentecost were
convicted of their sins at Peter's preaching and cried out,
"Brethren, what shall we do?" And Peter answered: "Repent, and be baptized every one of you in the name of Jesus
Christ for the forgiveness of your sins" (Acts 2:37, 38).

His reply recalls the challenge of John the Baptist: "Repent, for the kingdom of heaven is at hand." A continuing

mark of baptism is, therefore, its association with the problem of human sin. The baptismal candidate acutely senses his distance from the character of a holy God and turns back to that God and away from his egocentric life amid the pleasure of sin. He seeks forgiveness, and baptism signifies his willingness to cast off his own efforts to find it and to rely wholly on the way provided by a merciful Father.

So the confessional aspect of Christian baptism goes beyond the public avowal of Jesus Christ as Messiah and Lord. It signifies also the sinner's *need* of Jesus and his *faith* in Jesus as the One who can bring him the peace of forgiveness.

The precise role of baptism in relation to the saving work of Jesus Christ is not given extensive treatment in the New Testament. One passage, however, is significant for the issue—Romans 6:1-4. We must look at it carefully: "What shall we say then? Are we to continue in sin that grace may abound? By no means! How can we who died to sin still live in it? Do you not know that all of us who have been baptized into Christ Jesus were baptized into his death? We were buried therefore with him by baptism into death, so that as Christ was raised from the dead by the glory of the Father, we too might walk in newness of life."

We have often turned to these words to adduce the New Testament *mode* of baptism. Paul's imagery of death, burial, and resurrection, we have argued, clearly shows that baptism by immersion is intended. The candidate goes down into the watery grave and rises to newness of life. Sprinkling of water simply does not match the language Paul uses here.

Now the idea that New Testament baptism is by immersion is a sound one. The meaning of the word itself, the references to going down into and coming up out of the water (Acts 8:38; Matthew 3:16; Mark 1:10), and evidence from the ancient church baptistries all point to immersion as the primitive mode of baptism among Christians. It is not so certain, however, that Romans 6:1-4 gives the strong support for this mode that we often think. Note verse 5: "For if we have been united with him in a death like his, we shall certainly be united with him in a resurrection like his." The resurrection is yet future. What, then, of the imagery of dying and rising again as one comes out of the water?

Let us be clear on one point: Paul's concern here is not with the mode of baptism. (There was no dispute about this among the first Christians.) In fact, by coming to the passage primarily for apologetic reasons concerning the mode of baptism we fail to grasp the theology of baptism that he sets forth. Let us look at the passage again, seeking to discover the *meaning* of baptism.

The first two verses highlight two key sets of terms: sin/grace and death/life. These terms have been at the heart of Paul's discussion in Romans 5:12-21, where he has compared and contrasted Adam and Christ—the former is the source of universal sin and death, the latter of universal grace and life. After Adam's fall, sin abounded. Law could not remove it, could not bring man hope before God. But God had a solution. Abounding sin would be checked and overruled by grace more abounding in Jesus Christ (5:20). Whereas sin once reigned over mankind to death, so through Christ grace now reigns to eternal life (5:21).

Now, in Romans 6 to 8, Paul deals with the life of the Christian man or woman. He shows what Calvary means for the life of the believer in day-by-day experience. Over and over he comes back to the sets of sin/grace and death/life, arguing that since the child of God is under the reign of grace, he is no longer to be enslaved by sin (Romans 6:6, 7, 11, 14, 20, 21). The Christian lives a life of obedience as the Spirit of life works in and through him to do God's will (Romans 8:1-11).

So Paul's words about baptism in Romans 6:1-4 carry deep theological import. Paul will show us just what part baptism plays in this divine process whereby man is delivered from the bondage of sin and death to walk in righteousness and life.

The Christian, says Paul, has "died" to sin. But presumably his readers in Rome found that proposition difficult to accept, even as we do today. We are continually reminded in our everyday experience of the presence of sin—sin seems to be alive and well, if not indeed reigning as before.

To correct our understanding and to make his point unambiguous, Paul reminds us of our baptism: "Do you not know that all of us who have been baptized into Christ Jesus were baptized into his death?" (verse 3). Since he frames his point as a question, we cannot be sure whether Paul is jogging the memory of the Roman Christians or using a diplomatic form of imparting new teaching to them. The former possibility would be the more likely except that we do not have any parallel passage to this in the New Testament. Paul's meaning in these words, however, is more important than the previous knowledge of his hearers.

What, then, does Paul mean when he says "baptized into his death"? Clearly, the "died to sin" of verse 2 is proved by our baptism because we were baptized "into his death." In some way Paul is linking baptism with death— His and ours. Baptism marks a point of transition in relation to sin: It is our "death" to sin in signifying the radical turning from the old way to the new. But it is more, according to this reasoning. It also signifies our participation in His death, our incorporation into the crucifixion of the Lord. *When He died, we died!* Not just in the sense that He died in our place and for the sins of the world, because, says Paul, this incorporation is by baptism. Baptism indicates an identification of the *believer* (not of every person) with the death of Jesus.

These ideas are hard for us to grasp. Perhaps we, as modern people, find them more problematical than Paul's readers. For at least two hundred years the West has emphasized man the individual. So intense has been the concentration that our thoughts constantly fall into the pattern, and we tend to overlook or downgrade the fact that man is more than an individual. We forget that, beyond our own selves, we are bound to one another by subtle but nonetheless real cords. We are part of one another. "No man is an *Island*," as John Donne told us long ago. Indeed, the focus on individuality has led to impoverishment in human life and relations—hence the rise in recent years of encounter groups, sensitivity sessions, and so on.

While the Bible recognizes the individual and stresses personal accountability to God, it also tells us of our corporate personality. This idea is behind the passage about Christ and Adam (Romans 5:12-21; also 1 Corinthians 15:20-23). As we are all "in" Adam, who sums up and comprises the entire human race in his own person, so Christians are all "in" Christ. He is the head of the new humanity, the Progenitor of the Christian race. An arresting illustration of corporate personality in the Bible is found in the story of Abraham and Melchizedek. In Hebrews 7 we read that because Abraham paid tithe to Melchizedek, in a sense Levi, a descendant, also did (Hebrews 7:4-10).

Thus, in Romans 6:3 Paul describes the Christian's participation in the death of Jesus. The rite of baptism, he tells us, unites us with Christ so that we become identified with His death for sins. The mention of burial in verse 4—"we were buried ... with him by baptism into death"—underlines the *fact* of death. Burial signifies that a death has taken place: The person is really dead, not to be awakened from sleep or resuscitated. That is why the ancient Christian affirmation not only mentioned the death of Jesus but added that He was buried (1 Corinthians 15:4) and why the miracle of the raising of Lazarus, who had died and was buried, made such a profound impact (John 11).

So Paul throughout Romans 6 comes back to the *fact* of the Christian's death to sin: "Our old self was crucified with him" (verse 6); "he who has died . . ." (verse 7); "if we have died with Christ . . ." (verse 8); "consider yourselves dead to sin" (verse 11); "as men who have been brought from death" (verse 13).

Thus, we see the second confessional aspect of baptism. By baptism the believer enters into a solidarity with Jesus Christ his Lord—a solidarity in death. By going forward to the water he is publicly declaring his own sinfulness, his own guilt, his own death because of sins. And more: He declares his faith in the death of Jesus to solve the problem of his sins. By baptism he is joined with Christ in His crucifixion.

Implications

The confessional aspects of baptism that we have noticed in this chapter have an obvious implication for baptismal practice. If the candidate is to publicly demonstrate his recognition and acceptance of Jesus Christ as Lord and his identification with His death, he cannot be an infant. Repentance and faith both call for a maturity of mind and the ability to think for oneself and to make decisions. Infant baptism clearly cannot fulfill the meaning of baptism as confession.

What, then, should be the minimum age for baptism? Studies among groups that call for a maturation beyond infancy before baptism point to the twelve-to-fifteen-year age bracket as the peak period for baptism. Manifestly, young people will vary greatly in powers of understanding and the self-consciousness necessary for a personal decision for baptism. Occasionally we read of or meet Christians who are able to tell of their conversion at an early age, even before ten years. But such cases are rare.

Ministers and teachers of children frequently meet with requests for baptism from boys or girls of ten or eleven. To counsel them is a delicate task, requiring much tenderness and wisdom under the guidance of the Holy Spirit. On the one hand, the adult must try to safeguard against a hasty, emotional decision for baptism, one entered into primarily because of peer or parental pressures. He needs to be assured that the child recognizes the meaning and seriousness of baptism and has made a decision out of personal conviction. On the other hand, he has to beware of discouraging the sensitive feelings of the boy or girl. By teaching the child to put off baptism indefinitely, he may arrest spiritual development and put the child on a course where baptism will never take place. The years from ten to fifteen are marked by religious concern perhaps unsurpassed in its acuteness. We must be careful to foster it, not to dampen it.

We have been discussing the implications for baptismal practice, but the ideas of this chapter take us much further. Baptism as confession must cause each Christian to ponder at least three matters: its seriousness, the meaning of Christ's lordship today, and the radical nature of solidarity with His death.

Baptism is a *serious* rite. This is the preeminent fact to emerge. By being baptized, a person enacts a solemn decision that placards his own need and his understanding of and faith in Jesus Christ. Baptism is a public act, but it is not to be theatrical. It is a joyous experience, but it is not an entertainment.

Too often baptism is regarded lightly. Too often it is entered into without an awareness of its obligations as well as its privileges. The growing practice of rebaptism (for which the scantest Biblical support can be adduced) is distressing. If Christ is truly confessed at baptism, the rite should not be repeated. We must give urgent attention to the failure of candidates to grasp the meaning of baptism. Perhaps our desire to see people join the church through baptism has led us to diminish the seriousness of the act in our instruction. Christianity is not a club to be joined today and left tomorrow, perhaps with the thought of rejoining next week! Christ is not a political leader who may call forth our loyalty now but from whom we turn with the winds of change!

We mentioned something of what it meant to call Jesus Lord in the first century. The waves of persecution have long since subsided. At times there are advantages in our society in being known as a Christian. (Note how candidates for the Presidency are photographed at the Sunday services!) The name of Jesus has been appropriated by the popular song industry and by the publishing houses.

Yet it still means much if Jesus is really to be our Lord—if we are to go beyond the sugarcoated religion of the hit tunes, posters, and bumper stickers. To acknowledge Jesus as Lord means a renunciation, as it did from the beginning. It means a turning from the "stars" of the sports arena and the silver screen, from the headline-hunters and denizens of the pages of *People,* from adulation of the "brilliant" and the "beautiful." We *respect* beauty, intelligence, accomplishment—but we are not dazzled by them. Jesus alone is our *Lord.* He claims first and best place in our lives—always and forever. The relationship to Him is unique and undeviating. When Christians call Jesus Lord, they echo the first commandment of the Decalogue: "You shall have no other gods before me" (Exodus 20:3).

A Christian writer once described his relationship to Jesus as follows: When he was converted, it seemed as though Jesus came to him and said, "Frank, give Me the keys of your life." And he handed over the keys—but first slipped one of them off the key ring and put it in his pocket. So he lived as a Christian, enjoying the privileges of the new life. But always he was conscious of that one key, wearing a hole in his pocket. At last the day came when he took out the key and handed it over to Jesus. Now Jesus was Lord of all his being. Even so does the Christian grow in understanding of the lordship of Jesus.

Finally, baptism as confession speaks of the radical nature of solidarity with His death. It has always been difficult for mankind to admit that they cannot help themselves, that God must intervene and supply their religious need. Over and over religions have sprung up that prescribe various ways of pleasing God by a self-help course of action. To turn from self and cast oneself wholly upon divine grace is radical.

It is even more radical in today's world. Modern man has been fed the milk of self-sufficiency for so long that he finds it absurd to cast off his own resources. But baptism points to such an abandonment of the grasping ego. We are baptized into the *death* of Christ Jesus, becoming one with Him in the cross experience. That death signifies our total unworthiness, even as it looks to the new life that may arise out of it.

We have seen the deep meaning of baptism as a confession of Christ. By acknowledging Him publicly as Lord and by joining with Him in death, we find God's way of cleansing.

And as *we* confess Him, *He* confesses us. Recall the experience of Jesus as He came to the Jordan to be baptized by John. He went into the waters in order to fulfill all righteousness. He confessed, by so doing, His agreement with the mission of the Baptist and also His submission to the divine will. And as He came up out of the water, the voice from heaven said: "This is my beloved Son, with whom I am well pleased" (Matthew 3:17). And the Spirit of God descended like a dove upon Him. Thus did the Father supply His confession to the person and act of Jesus.

Even so will baptism today be accompanied by divine blessings. To each the Father says again, "This is my beloved son or daughter, with whom I am well pleased." And the Spirit of God again will descend. These topics will form the basis of our discussion in the next chapter.

4

Cleansed to New Life

In the previous chapter we saw that Christian baptism points to death. But death is not the final outworking of the symbol. The radical character of baptism, shown by Paul's emphasis on burial to indicate certainty of death, is to produce *new life*.

Professor Eliade, in *Patterns in Comparative Religion*, discusses the enduring symbolism of water. He reminds us of "the face of the waters" in the primal chaos before Creation. He points out that water represents the forces of dissolution, the return to the womb of time, the breaking up of order and structure. This is true for the individual who returns to the waters by immersion, as well as for the cosmos itself when it was swept by the Deluge.

But out of this dissolution come new order and new life. Just as the first waters were the fount of our world, so the return to chaos symbolized by deluge or immersion is but the way to a new world and a new existence. "Water symbolizes the whole of potentiality; it is *fons et origo,* the source of all possible existence" (Mircea Eliade, *op. cit.,* p. 188).

Only as the old is dissolved, only as the primal chaos returns, can the new existence be fashioned. Thus, death is the womb of life.

We must press the point: *Only as there is first death can*

the new life issue forth. We are not involved here in matters of degree—good and better—or slight changes in life-style. No, the Biblical language points to a metamorphosis, a fundamental breaking of behavior patterns with the institution of new ones. We must not diminish the radical nature of the symbolism. We must face it and seek to understand it.

Another way of expressing these ideas is in terms of rites of passage. Gail Sheehy in her popular *Passages* has reminded us of the changes in our thinking that come with the various stages of life. Baptism points to such a transition—one that is, however, more sudden and far reaching. Baptism is the transition, the rite of passage, from the old to the new. It leads the old into *death* so that life—a new life—may be born:

$$\text{Old Life} \xrightarrow[\text{Death}]{\text{Baptism}} \text{New Life}$$

We must explore the nature of this transition. Does the New Testament in fact set out such a dramatic change of life in association with Christian baptism? Does baptism in itself have the power to effect sweeping changes in personality and behavior? How can the ideas of the New Testament be brought together with our modern understanding of man? We must wrestle with these issues in this chapter. Our study will lead us to the following aspects: the new birth, the new life, the Holy Spirit, the role of baptism, and implications for modern man.

The New Birth

The third chapter of John is a classic. In the meeting of Jesus and Nicodemus we hear more than a discussion of religious truth—we learn that the religion of the Nazarene confronts all naturalistic processes of thought and calls for utter transformation. Man, said Jesus, must be "born again."

Jesus did not explain in terms of modern psychology how the new birth takes place. His words here rather deal with three aspects of it: its factuality, its necessity, and its agency.

"That which is born of the flesh is flesh, and that which is born of the Spirit is spirit," He declared (verse 6). Here Jesus lays out unequivocally two levels of human existence. The first is the level of "flesh" and is common to all mankind. In contrast, the level of "spirit" is held out to the one who hears and believes the words of Jesus. Just as we commence life in the world through the avenue of human birth, so we enter upon the higher life by a transition that He calls the new birth.

Jesus' terminology points up the nature of the change involved. To be born anew means entering upon a new course of life at a point in time. Whatever continuities we may be able to locate, it is clear that a radical transformation has taken place.

Further, such a marked change is necessary, teaches Jesus. The life that is lived on the level of flesh can never enter the kingdom of God. No disciplining; no educating; no gritting of the teeth; no blood, sweat, and tears; no striving can perfect the flesh. One does not grow up to the level of spirit. He is born anew to it. There is no other way.

The transformation, then, does not come about by human effort. Significantly the Greek word translated "anew" or "again" (anōthen) also means "from above." The new birth comes by the divine agency of God's Spirit. Like the wind ("wind" and "spirit" both translate the same Greek word pneuma)—silent, unobtrusive, unseen—the Spirit of God "blows" on the heart. The effects are visible, if the process is not: A new birth comes about. "But to all who received him, who believed in his name, he gave power to become children of God; who were born, not of blood nor of the will of the flesh nor of the will of man, but of God" (John 1:12, 13).

For our study of baptism, the most interesting verse in John 3 is verse 5: "Jesus answered, 'Truly, truly, I say to you, unless one is born of water and the Spirit, he cannot enter the kingdom of God.' " Here in a direct and unambiguous manner Jesus associates the process of the new birth with baptism. He seems to be saying: The invisible work of the Spirit will be matched by a visible work of the believer. Just as the act of going forward to the water gives concrete expression to one's inner acknowledgment of the person and death of Jesus, so the immersion in the water becomes the transition to new life in the Lord.

John 3:1-21 will always be central in any discussion of the nature of Christian experience. And verse 5 must remain a central verse to show the deep significance that our religion attaches to baptism. From it alone we know that baptism is more than a form, a routine. It moves in the orbit of death and life, of the transforming power of God's presence.

It seems clear, then, that the new life of Christians is not something which slowly infuses them. It is something that he or she enters upon. The Christian is born into it. And baptism marks the transition from the old to the new. The waters represent at once dissolution and regeneration.

Let us see how the New Testament writers further set out this new life of the Christian with regard to baptism.

The New Life

When the New Testament speaks of a new birth and a new life in Christ, how extensive is the effect? Is there mainly and merely a God-orientation, a change in spirituality? Or does the transformation extend to the total behavior?

A graphic passage from Paul's first letter to Corinth supplies the answer. "Do you not know that the unrighteous will not inherit the kingdom of God? Do not be deceived; neither the immoral, nor idolaters, nor adulterers, nor sexual perverts, nor thieves, nor the greedy, nor drunkards, nor revilers, nor robbers will inherit the kingdom of God. And such were some of you. But you were washed, you were sanctified, you were justified in the name of the Lord Jesus Christ and in the Spirit of our God" (1 Corinthians 6:9-11).

The text staggers us. Paul has painted a grim picture of life in ancient Corinth—as grim as we can find anywhere in the entire Bible. Indeed, Corinth was a byword in the ancient world. "To Corinthianize" meant to live a life of moral abandonment. Corinth for centuries had been a center for the worship of Venus-Aphrodite. This worship involved thousands of "sacred" prostitutes. Truly, if Christianity could succeed in Corinth, it could succeed anywhere in the ancient world.

And it *did* take root in Corinth. The first believers there were not outsiders who took up residence in the city. After Paul lists the vices of the people of Corinth, he reminds his readers: *"And such were some of you."* The gospel, however, had dramatically changed their lives. Formerly they were far from the kingdom of God. Their profligate ways demonstrated the fact. But now they were *washed* (surely a reference to the cleansing signified by baptism), *justified* (acquitted in heaven's law court), and *sanctified* (set apart as God's own people in the midst of a pagan society).

Perhaps no other text of the New Testament so well illustrates the ethical implications of the new life. Clearly, the person who believes in Jesus and publicly confesses Him in baptism undergoes a radical change. This transformation is twofold. On its Godward side it means that he or she has come into a saving relation with God, that sins have been forgiven, and that the status of a child of the heavenly Father has begun. In its manward side it means that the careless living of the past is put aside. The new person now lives for the glory of God.

The entire New Testament underlines the fact and characteristics of the new life. First one aspect, then another—sometimes the Godward, sometimes the manward, varying with the needs and problems of the Christians from place to place—comes to the fore. So the New Testament over and over reaffirms the words of Jesus: "You must be born again."

Already in this chapter we have mentioned the Holy Spirit. We recall Jesus' statement that unless a man is born *of water and of the Spirit* he cannot see the kingdom of God (John 3:5). Now we must look more carefully at this matter. What is the role of the Spirit in the new birth and new life?

The Role of the Holy Spirit

Jesus' discourse with Nicodemus pointed out the decisive part of the Holy Spirit in the new birth. Just as we are helpless at the moment of our physical birth, so no person by force of will or effort can effect his own new birth. The new life comes "from above" from its inception. Only as the Spirit with His quiet "blowing" works upon human nature will "flesh" be left behind and "spirit" come about. But if the will does not resist the Spirit's influence, the change from "flesh" to "spirit" *will* take place: Man is born again.

Not only does the Holy Spirit effect the new birth, however. The new life itself derives from the continual, prevailing presence of the Spirit. It is life *in the Spirit*.

The Baptist, we remember, had prophesied this. About the Coming One he predicted: "He will baptize you with the Holy Spirit and with fire" (Matthew 3:11). The entire New Testament witnesses to the fulfillment of his words. As the Master Himself was endued with the Spirit at the time of His baptism, so those baptized in His name receive the power of the Spirit for the new life.

The Book of Acts constantly makes the point. And the nineteenth chapter records an especially illuminating example. At Ephesus Paul came upon a group of John the Baptist's followers. Apparently they had left Palestine after having been baptized by John and had not heard of Jesus and His baptism. They had not received the Holy Spirit. In fact, they had not even heard of the Holy Spirit. On hearing of Jesus as the fulfillment of John's predictions, they were baptized in His name (Acts 19:1-5). And immediately they received the Holy Spirit (verses 6, 7).

The passage is interesting on at least two counts. First, it shows the long-standing influence of the Baptist—this incident occurred more than twenty years after his death. (As we noticed earlier, there is evidence of a John the Baptist sect that opposed early Christianity. Remnants of it continue to this day in Mesopotamia.) Second, it shows one point of strong contrast between the two baptisms—the giving of the Holy Spirit.

The New Testament is the age of the Spirit. We encounter a mysterious element here. We do not fully grasp all the reasons why this should be so, even as the nature of the Spirit Himself lies beyond our complete comprehension. Certainly Old Testament times were not devoid of the Spirit's presence and functioning. His work, however, is much less prominent and is mentioned in connection with individuals here and there (for example, Exodus 31:1-11). According to the Gospel of John, Jesus predicted the age of the Spirit, a time when His activity would be manifested much beyond that of the old era (John 7:37-39). We find hints as to the reason for the outpouring of the Spirit: The Spirit was to carry on the work of the incarnate Son, bringing His words to remembrance and glorifying Him (John 14:26; 15:26; 16:8-11, 14); Pentecost was the evidence of the triumph of Jesus in His death and resurrection (Acts 2:32, 33).

New Testament proclamation has the basic character of witness. That witness centers in two affirmations—one objective and one subjective. Objectively, Christians declare the fact of Jesus' resurrection. Subjectively, they declare the certainty of the Holy Spirit in their personal experiences and in the collective life of the church.

The New Testament is a book of great excitement. Something *had happened!* The early Christians could look back to a life filled with the glory of God, a death that redeemed the world, and a resurrection that broke the bonds of death. Something *was happening!* Their Lord had left them, but they felt the Divine Presence among them. That Spirit of Christ had transformed them and had turned unlearned fishermen into apostles who traversed the globe and turned it upside down. He had not only made them anew, regenerated them, but He also continually supplied the stream of new life.

The Role of Baptism

This chapter has highlighted the transforming nature of the gospel. The new birth means a change from death to life, from darkness to light, from slavery to freedom, from enmity to peace, from aloneness to security. This change starts with the inner man, touching the very fount of existence, and it pervades at last the total being, so that behavior is altered beyond recognition. One can only say that the Christian has become a new person.

All this is clear. But now we must raise the critical question for understanding baptism: Precisely *how* does baptism enter into the new birth and new life?

Perhaps we can best answer the question by locating the opposing poles of proposed solutions. On one hand, we might argue that, since Jesus told of the need to be "born of water," the rite itself possesses a transforming power. Pushed to the limit, this idea would teach that the baptismal water in and of itself works regeneration. The early church father Tertullian wrote of baptism in such terms. He argued that from Creation, waters were imbued with extraordinary power.

On the other hand we might contend that baptism has minimal consequence in itself. After all, the dying thief whom Jesus declared would be in Paradise with Him was not baptized. Baptism is no more than a public declaration, a witness to all that one has decided to follow Jesus.

It seems as if the New Testament teaching about baptism assigns it a role somewhere between these poles. Clearly, the New Testament does not suggest a mechanical power in the rite itself. Never does it associate a magical or superstitious quality to the cleansing water. Baptism, it shows, is the outworking of a personal *faith* in Jesus Christ as Saviour and Lord. That faith comes to concrete expression in the public confession which constitutes baptism. And we have seen that the New Testament declares the Holy Spirit to be the agent of regeneration and renewal.

But baptism is also entered into for a *personal* benefit. The New Testament cannot support the idea that it is primarily a witness to the assembled onlookers. The association of baptism with new birth and regeneration and the receiving of the Holy Spirit shows that much more is involved. Baptism is the door to the new life, the outworking of faith, the transition from the old to the new. When we go forward in baptism, God comes down to bless. Without baptism, said Jesus, one will not enter the kingdom of God—but we *do* enter it at the moment of baptism.

Our reflections here deserve more extensive treatment. Toward the close of the book we shall return to this issue as we take into account our overall study of the meaning of Christian baptism (Chapter 6).

Implications for Modern Man

The New Testament world was a dynamic one. Sinners became saints, persecutors became preachers, traitors became trustworthy. God was felt to be close, experienced within. He made individuals new and raised up a new religion.

But how do we move from the first century to the twentieth? How shall we relate the ideas of this chapter to our modern understanding of man? What do these things mean to us today?

We continue to hear the news that *man can change*. This is good news indeed, for often we feel helpless as modern people. Science has pointed out the ways in which we are influenced by heredity and environment—the argument rages only over which is decisive. B. F. Skinner's *Beyond Freedom and Dignity* argues that we are totally conditioned. Our so-called decisions are entirely predictable if the influences that impinge upon us can be identified. We feel the pressures of modern life, the huge impact of Madison Avenue, the persuasive powers of television, radio, and the printed word. But the New Testament says, "You have enough freedom to change." Freedom is not total, but it is sufficient. *Man can change!*

But the change—and it speaks of radical change, a life transformed in thinking, desiring, willing, acting, loving— does not come about by our modern methods. The agency of radical change is itself radical: It is God! None other can change a person into a new being.

When the New Testament brings in the God-factor, science must remain mute. The empirical method deals only with the natural, with that which can be grasped by sensory perception. It cannot discuss God and His agency. It can, at best, stand aside to observe if, in fact, radical change occurs. But it has nothing to predict about the possibility of such.

And Christian witness now, as anciently, is that the radical change still occurs. God's hand is not shortened that He cannot save. His grace is as mighty now as when the ancients felt its power. Men and women walking the streets can say from the heart: "I was down and out. I was crushed and beaten by life. I was a slave to the bottle, the cigarette, the joint. But

God's presence has made me into a new person. My life is totally altered. My thinking, my hopes, my aspirations are altogether transformed. He has made me over anew."

All who seek to be baptized in the name of Jesus Christ should be conscious of God's life-changing power. They may have been brought up within the Christian fold, so that the dramatic turning to Christ is not in evidence. Nor should they wait until they can point to the development of a character like God's—the church is not a club for the already perfected! What is needed, however, is the sense of God's power in the life, coming down to take control so that Jesus has truly become Lord of the life.

The subject of the Holy Spirit often causes some uneasiness among Christians. When John Wesley began to preach in the diocese of Bristol, Bishop Butler rebuked him with: "To pretend to extraordinary revelations from the Holy Ghost is a horrid thing, a very horrid thing." Christians today are not likely to call Paul's teachings about the Holy Spirit in personal Christian living "a very horrid thing," but they are wary of the area. They feel alarmed by what they see and hear in the name of the Spirit and by the claims that are often made from a basis of the Christianity in the Book of Acts.

Unfortunately the Holy Spirit often has not been well represented by those who claim His presence. We have come to associate His coming with spectacular phenomena in which the kingly power of reason is thrust aside and an unpredictable emotionalism takes the chair. Is this the meaning of the New Testament doctrine of the Spirit?

Not in my judgment. Jesus, we recall, used the illustration of the wind. The Spirit works silently, unobtrusively, steadily, to do His work. Nowhere does the New Testament teach that the receiving of the Spirit must be accompanied by dramatic manifestations such as speaking in tongues (some Christian groups err greatly at this point). Indeed, Paul rebuked the church at Corinth for its excesses in the name of the

Spirit. He told them that disorder, confusion, and lack of understanding are not the work of the Spirit (1 Corinthians 14:26-33). Instead he pointed them to the "better way"—the way of love. This harmonizes with his instruction elsewhere about the fruit of the Spirit.

We should not, therefore, emphasize a physical manifestation of the Holy Spirit at the time of baptism. Rather, it is the day-by-day influence of the Spirit, as He molds the new life more and more into the image of the Lord, that shows His presence in the life.

So far in our study of Christian baptism we have looked at the topic in terms of the *individual* who becomes a Christian. We saw that baptism involves confession—of Christ as Lord and as one with His death (Chapter 3). And we have seen here that it is the bridge to new life in Him.

But baptism also is the door to the church. Baptism has a corporate meaning that goes beyond individual confession and benefit. We will explore this area in Chapter 5.

5

Cleansed for the Body of Christ

The twentieth century is the age of the individual par excellence. In our day those currents of thought that the Enlightenment set in motion nearly three centuries ago have converged and swollen to flood tide. Ours is the era of the "person" and the "star," of personality and psychology—the late shoot in the tree of science that has outgrown the original branches. National and societal concerns have given way to the individual's pleasures, rights, and desires. Doing your own thing is the catchcry. Self-realization is the goal. No wonder the task of government grows more difficult by the year.

Religion has also been affected by this flow of ideas. Christianity, like every religion, is clothed in the ideas of the times. As a result, man-centered theologies have developed—especially in this century. The thought of Rudolf Bultmann, for instance, focused on man's quest for "authentic existence," but American theology in the 1960s went even further in the so-called "death of God" theology.

Nor has popular religion been unaffected. The Jesus movement and the charismatic Christianity of the 1970s have stressed *individual* contact with God. God is to be felt, experienced. His Spirit is to overflow the Christian, loosing the tongue and manifesting gifts of healing and exorcism.

The Bible would tell us that we are *more* than individuals, however. We are bound up with each other by the invisible cords of the bundle of life. Although God holds each man or woman separately accountable, the Bible also instructs us in *corporate* personality. We are part of one another, just as we are part of those who have gone before. This conception lies behind Paul's "in Adam" and "in Christ" expressions (Romans 5; 1 Corinthians 15). It also explains the puzzling idea of Hebrews 7:4-10 in which Levi, before he had been born, is said to have paid tithes to Melchizedek through his ancestor Abraham.

Baptism likewise has a corporate dimension. Becoming a Christian involves more than individual acceptance and confession of Jesus as Saviour and Lord. Its orbit is wider than the circle of individual privileges and blessings that we have noted in the previous two chapters. Baptism is inseparably linked to the church. By baptism we become part of the body of Christ. When we try to separate individual Christianity from the church, we miss the mark of the New Testament evidence. Just as there are individual privileges and responsibilities, so there are corporate ones.

We will take up the corporate involvements of baptism by considering in turn the *status* of those baptized into Christ, their corporate *privileges,* and their corporate *responsibilities.*

Christian Status

The New Testament writers employed many metaphors or models to highlight the status of Christians. We shall look briefly at six of them.

1. When Paul wrote to the church at Corinth, he addressed his remarks to the "sanctified" ones, that is, the "saints." The term is doubly surprising. First, we usually reserve sainthood for a very rare type of person. Even in the Roman Catholic Church, canonization takes place only

years after death. Second, the idea of saints in Corinth
boggles the mind. Corinth was notorious for its moral rot-
tenness.

But Paul wrote further on this point: "Such [belonging
to the category of vices listed] were some of you. But you
were washed, you were sanctified" (1 Corinthians 6:11).
There is no doubt about his point: The Christians in
Corinth were saints! Indeed, Paul used this term fairly
often to describe New Testament Christians. We need to
look at it closely to see its original meaning.

The word itself, literally "sanctified one," had its roots
in a worship context. We recall the oft-repeated words of
Leviticus: "Be holy, for I am holy" (11:44, 45; 19:2; 20:7,
26). The Israelites were set apart, cleansed for Yahweh's
service. So in Paul's day Christians belonged to God. In a
world in rebellion against Him, they had acknowledged
Him as Lord. They were consecrated to His service, dedicated for His glory. So they were the "saints."

2. Another model of New Testament Christianity was
drawn from family relations. In many places the New Testament calls us God's sons and daughters (for example, 2
Corinthians 6:18). The idea goes back to Jesus Himself, who
constantly spoke of God as Father and taught us to so
address Him in our prayers (Matthew 6:9). The idea is clear
and appealing: As baptized people we are part of the family
of God. The incomparable parable of the prodigal son (Luke
15:11-32) is based on it.

Paul, however, sharpened the point. He insisted that
formerly, without Christ, we were orphans. We were alone
in a forbidding universe, lost in the vastnesses of space. We
were strangers, far off, without hope. But Christianity has
come as adoption. No longer are we aliens. We belong! We
have status as full-fledged members of the family of God in
heaven and earth (Romans 8:15-17; Galatians 4:4-7). Paul
even taught the believers to use a term of childlike affection

and simplicity when speaking to God: Abba—literally "Daddy."

3. We have already been using the word *church*, and now we should take a closer look at it. The Greek word is *ekklēsia* and literally means an assembly of people summoned for a particular purpose. That purpose may be secular in nature (for example, Acts 19:41). As used for Christians, however, the accent fell on the *community* of believers gathered by God through Christ. There were local assemblies, as at Rome, Corinth, and Thessalonica, but the church was more than this assembly. It existed prior to the people's coming together for worship. So the church was commonly called the church *of God* (Acts 20:28; 1 Corinthians 1:2; 10:32—among others) and sometimes "the church . . . in God the [or "our"] Father and the Lord Jesus Christ" (1 Thessalonians 1:1; 2 Thessalonians 1:1).

How high is the status of the baptized person! He is separated for God. He is part of God's family. He is a member of the community that embraces heaven and earth.

4. A fourth way of expressing Christian status was in terms of the people of God. The link with the Old Testament is very strong here: The church corresponds to Israel of old. So we read of the "Israel of God" (Galatians 6:16), of the "new covenant" (Hebrews 8:8-10), of scattered Christians as "the twelve tribes in the Dispersion" (James 1:1; see also 1 Peter 1:1), of the spiritual sons of Abraham (Galatians 3:29), of spiritual circumcision (Romans 2:29), and of the New Jerusalem (Revelation 21). The Book of Ephesians rings with this idea. Ephesians is hardly a letter—it is more a hymn of the church of Christ. And one of its great themes is that Jesus Christ broke down the wall of partition between Jew and Gentile so that Gentiles now can have full access in the Israel of God (2:11-21).

In some places the *wandering* people of God furnished the model. Like Israel in the wilderness, God's people are on the move. They are on the way to the Promised Land, and they live by faith, not by sight (Hebrews 3:7–4:11; 11:13-16).

5. The idea of a new race formed the basis for yet another model. This striking conception speaks with unusual power to the people of our times when racial and ethnic division are often so explosive. Paul provided the two classic passages that lay out the metaphor: "Then as one man's trespass led to condemnation for all men, so one man's act of righteousness leads to acquittal and life for all men. For as by one man's disobedience many were made sinners, so by one man's obedience many will be made righteous" (Romans 5:18, 19).

"For as by a man came death, by a man has come also the resurrection of the dead. For as in Adam all die, so also in Christ shall all be made alive" (1 Corinthians 15:21, 22).

No wonder the ancient world crumbled before the onslaught of Christianity! The new religion dissolved the walls of partition between man and man. No longer would a person be first a Jew, a Greek, a Roman, or an Egyptian. He would be a Christian—a member of the Christian race! The church of God in our day badly needs to hear again this word of the transforming gospel.

6. We come at last to what is perhaps the most arresting New Testament image of all—that of the body. Once again Paul has provided it: "For just as the body is one and has many members, and all the members of the body, though many, are one body, so it is with Christ. For by one Spirit we were all baptized into one body—Jews or Greeks, slaves or free—and all were made to drink of one Spirit. For the body does not consist of one member but of many." "Now you are the body of Christ and individually members of it" (1 Corinthians 12:12-14, 27; see also Romans 12:4, 5 and Ephesians 4:4-6, 15, 16).

This passage provides us with the most clear-cut statement of the corporate implications of baptism. A person is not simply baptized as an act between him and God. He is baptized *"into one body."* This rite gives voice to the confession of Christ and seals it and links the candidate inexorably with His church.

The metaphor of the body suggests both unity and differentiation. There is no loss of individuality. Rather, each person has a particular contribution to make to the cause of God. Yet there is a *fusing* of individual efforts so that the community at large may be most benefited. We shall return to this matter later in the chapter.

We see, then, that a Christian has an exalted place: He or she is attached to God in a close relationship and for a divine purpose. But we have also noticed that this status must not be construed in an individualizing manner. As God's sons and daughters, we are members of a *family*. As His saints, we belong to a community, a consecrated people, the counterpart of ancient Israel. As a new creation in Christ, we are part of the new humanity. As an individual in Christ, we are a member of His body.

Thus, baptism in Christ is always the gateway to participation in His church. We turn now to consider the privileges of such membership.

Incorporation Into the Body: Privileges

Incorporation into the body of Christ brings matchless privileges. Those today who would bad-mouth the church—whether from outside or inside—would do well to note them.

The church, first of all, is a place of *belonging*. In God's ideal it is to be a caring, loving community. Here differences of education and bank account, of skin and IQ, are transcended. Old and young, male and female, black and white—each is important for his or her own sake as a member of the body of Christ. Paul wrote: "In Christ Jesus you are all sons of God, through faith. For as many of you as were baptized into Christ have put on Christ. There is neither Jew nor Greek, there is neither slave nor free, there is neither male nor female; for you are all one in Christ Jesus" (Galatians 3:26-28).

The body of Christ says to each Christian, "You are important. You are part of the family of God. You are joined to Christ and to other Christians in a mysterious, but real, union. You are indispensable in God's plan for the body, and the body is indispensable for you."

Unfortunately, the ideal of Galatians 3:26, 27 often goes unrealized. Over the course of the centuries the church at times has sacrificed Paul's pattern on the altar of economic or political expediency. Sometimes people outside the church have shown a greater sensitivity to human equality and injustice than the leaders of the church.

A closely related benefit will be that of *fellowship*. The New Testament word is *koinōnia*, a participation, a sharing, a communion. *Koinōnia* has two aspects: a God/man fellowship and a man/man sharing.

Paul wrote of the first when he told the Corinthian believers that they "were called into the fellowship of his Son, Jesus Christ our Lord" (1 Corinthians 1:9). He spoke of the bread and the wine of the Lord's Supper as a sharing in the body and blood of Christ (1 Corinthians 10:16). The apostolic benediction (2 Corinthians 13:14) included "the fellowship of the Holy Spirit." Likewise John spoke of "fellowship with him" (1 John 1:6).

But Paul and John likewise spoke of the *koinōnia* that Christians enjoy with each other. "We know that as you share in our sufferings, you will also share in our comfort," wrote Paul to the Corinthian Christians, in 2 Corinthians 1:7. He reminded the Galatians that the apostles in Jerusalem extended to him and Barnabas "the right hand of fellowship" (Galatians 2:9). John can state: "If we walk in the light, as he is in the light, we have fellowship with one another" (1 John 1:7). In 1 John 1:3 the two aspects of fellowship flow together: "That which we have seen and heard we proclaim also to you, so that you may have fellowship with us; and our fellowship is with the Father and with his Son Jesus Christ."

Paul's most extensive presentation of the church as the body of Christ (in 1 Corinthians 12:4-31) brought out this sympathetic sharing among the members. Every member is vital to the total functioning of the body, he argued, so that there must be no consideration of superiority or inferiority. And just as we hurt if our tooth or toe hurts, so "if one member suffers, all suffer together; if one member is honored, all rejoice together" (verse 26).

A third privilege that derives from incorporation into the body of Christ is worship. Worship, of course, covers a broad spectrum. In its widest sense it embraces every act of life. Even work becomes worship when we dedicate it to God. Worship also embraces the individual's communion with the divine—those moments of silent aloneness when no other human is present to intervene between man and his Maker. But worship has corporate sense too. The Book of Revelation in particular sets out worship in these terms. Throughout the writing the action is interrupted by anthems and hallelujahs, by outbursts of praise and adoration from saints and angels (for example, 7:9-12; 11:15-18; 15:2-4; 16:5-7; 19:1-8).

The reception of spiritual gifts is a final benefit accruing from baptism. We place it here in the discussion of the body of Christ because that is where Paul located it. To sever spiritual gifts from the living connection with the church can lead only to misunderstanding and misuse.

There is much talk about spiritual gifts among Christians today. This is a healthy development and can lead the church to a new dynamism. Unfortunately, however, the emphasis at times falls heavily on the individual and *his* gifts. We are in danger of falling into the error of the Corinthians. They were "not lacking in any spiritual gift" (1 Corinthians 1:7), but they were abusing their gifts. We read of dissension, factionalism, pride, arrogance, disorder. There seems to have been strong rivalry between the prophets and the glossolalists in particular (1 Corinthians 14). Paul felt constrained to devote a large section of his letter (1 Corinthians 12-14) to setting matters straight.

He lays out the relation of the gifts to the body of Christ in chapter 12. Spiritual gifts come from the one and same Spirit, he points out (verses 4-11). Man should not boast of them, for they are not of his making. Earlier in the letter Paul had written: "What have you that you did not receive? If then you received it, why do you boast as if it were not a gift?" (1 Corinthians 4:7). And because *all* gifts come from the same Spirit, we must not categorize them in terms of value. Indeed, Paul goes on, *every* gift is important, just as each part of the body is vital to its effective functioning (12:14-26).

What, then, is the purpose of the gifts? Verse 7 sums up Paul's answer: "for the common good." Instead of promoting comparisons, rivalries, jealousies, and feelings of individual superiority, the gifts are to build up the church.

A place to belong, a place of fellowship, a place to worship, a place to build and to be built up by spiritual gifts—great indeed are the privileges of incorporation into the body of Christ!

Incorporation Into the Body: Responsibilities

But privilege brings responsibility, and great privileges carry great responsibilities. Jesus said: "Every one to whom much is given, of him will much be required" (Luke 12:48).

It calls, at the least, for a way of life that will correspond with the high status conferred on Christians. If we are sons and daughters of the living God, His separated ones for a holy purpose, our lives should show a difference.

So throughout the New Testament we hear the refrain of the ethical imperative. Salvation is a free gift, and we now are children of the Heavenly King—so remember who you are! Live out your high calling! This is not a legalism, an arid turning again to man's works of righteousness in the futile effort to satisfy God. No. Salvation is all of God. But that salvation is transforming: It makes us into children of light. Grace bestowed on the individual makes him over anew. If no change occurs, he has frustrated God's purpose for his life. This is not a perfectionism, a soul-destroying counting of minutiae. Instead it is the recognition of the new humanity in Jesus Christ.

It would be superfluous to trace Jesus' ethical concerns through each of the Gospels. In fact, they pervade the New Testament writings. Even Paul in his letters to Rome and Galatia, which are often appealed to (and rightly so) for the glorious truth of justification by faith, devotes lengthy portions to instruction in practical godliness. "I appeal to you therefore, brethren, by the mercies of God, to present your bodies as a living sacrifice, holy and acceptable to God, which is your spiritual worship" (Romans 12:1). "For you were called to freedom, brethren; only do not use your freedom as an opportunity for the flesh, but through love be servants of one another. For the whole law is fulfilled in one word, 'You shall love your neighbor as yourself' " (Galatians 5:13, 14).

The divine ideal for the church is best set forth in Ephesians 5:25, 26. Paul used the marriage relationship as a figure for the love of Christ for His people. Further, he brought in the baptismal figure. It is as though the church were being baptized. And the divine plan emerges: The self-giving of Jesus was for the body, the communion, to bring it into being, to present it at last as a spotless, beautiful bride. "Husbands, love your wives, as Christ loved the church and gave himself up for her, that he might sanctify her, having cleansed her by the washing of water with the word" (Ephesians 5:25, 26).

But this ethical imperative is not a call to introspection. Christians are not to shut themselves away from the world with its cares and problems, for that is where the people are. Nor is the Christian ethic merely an overcoming of sin.

The note of ethical concern is blended by one of Christian *witness*. Because we are members of the body of Christ and because that is such a blessed privilege, we let others know about it. Early Christian preaching always partook of this character. It was not a discussion or a discourse, an argument or an allegory. The apostles in Acts knew of two great truths—the living Christ of the Resurrection and the Holy Spirit within. So they could not keep silent: "We cannot but speak of what we have seen and heard" (Acts 4:20).

The risen Lord has given Christians their marching orders. As they have become disciples, so they are to make disciples. As they have been taught, so they are to teach. As they have been baptized, so they are to baptize. The church is not a club for the elite, a closed society of "the perfect," who indulge in mutual scrutiny and congratulation. Christ meant it to be a universal fellowship, extending to earth's farthest bounds and inviting all men everywhere to come into its circle. Nor will its word of witness ever cease as long as its Lord is separated from it. To the end of the age its mission must go forward.

We have been referring, of course, to Matthew 28:18-20: "And Jesus came and said to them, 'All authority in heaven and on earth has been given to me. Go therefore and make disciples of all nations, baptizing them in the name of the

Father and of the Son and of the Holy Spirit, teaching them to observe all that I have commanded you; and lo, I am with you always, to the close of the age.' " It comes with particular helpfulness to us as we endeavor to see the role of baptism in the mission of the church. There are four key verbs in verse 19—go, make [disciples], baptize, and teach. As we look at the original construction of the Greek, we observe that the wording is such that three verbs cluster around and serve the fourth—"make disciples." That is, Jesus is saying: "Make all nations my disciples: go, baptize, teach." Baptism is part of the disciplining of the world.

We now can grasp more clearly the role of the Christian. Our study in this section has shown that incorporation into the body of Christ cannot leave us the same. Instead of being conformed, we are transformed! (See Romans 12:2.) There is a new hatred of sin and evil, a continual sorrow for sin, and a turning from it. (So repentance characterizes the lifelong experience of the Christian.) There is an outflowing of living concern and mercy to all around us, especially to those who are members of the church, but not exclusively to them. And there is a sharing of the Good News of the salvation brought us by Christ and available to "whosoever will."

It is obvious, then, that the New Testament ideal brings the individual member into the closest relationship possible with the church. He is part of it, a member of the body. It is his church. He is interested in its health, welfare, reputation, and growth.

This conception would severely correct much Christian life in our day. We see a strange pitting of Christian individuals or groups against "the church," in terms of "we" and "they." At times Christians snipe at the church. Many are indifferent, supercritical, and even destructive. Such attitudes are incredible if we would let the New Testament image of the body of Christ sink in. Does anyone have a hand that works against his body? Self-inflicted pain is a form of mental sickness. Christians who work against the church exhibit spiritual sickness.

Baptism, then, with peculiar force tells us *who* we are and *what* we are. It reveals to us our lofty status and our magnificent privileges as members of the church. But it also unfolds our role as part of Christ's body. Only as we see how highly He regards the church will we value it, support it, and throw our weight behind its unfinished task.

6

Sacrament or Symbol?

We have now finished our investigation of the Biblical data relative to Christian baptism. We have seen how the rite grew out of, and is based on, the baptism of John. We found that it centers in the confession of Jesus Christ, with confession embracing a public act of avowal of Jesus coupled with a denial of one's own sufficiency before God. Baptism signifies a radical change in living. And it brings with it corporate benefits and obligations, as well as individual ones.

Our concerns in this chapter are general and holistic. We have looked at baptism in detail. Now we want to stand back and see the subject in entirety. We wish to grasp its total significance in the Christian religion. Just how important is baptism? What should one legitimately expect to occur at baptism?

These are difficult but vital issues. In order to come to grips with them we need to cast our mental net into new waters. First, we shall cast it over the right side of the boat, into the waters of history. We shall trace the course of baptism in Christian thought to see how it came to be regarded as a sacrament. Then we shall throw our net on the left side, into the waters of symbolism. It will help us see the nature and function of religious symbols so that we can grasp what we mean when we call baptism a symbol.

This study will bring the wheel full circle, because we shall be drawn back to our studies of the first chapter.

The Development of Sacramental Baptism

The development of thinking that led Christians to view baptism as a sacrament is long and involved. Although there are some gaps in our knowledge, the overall picture is clear—and fascinating. It revolves around two words: the Greek *mustērion*, literally "mystery"; and the Latin *sacramentum*, "sacrament."

The word *mustērion* probably derives from a Greek word that meant "to close." That is, the mouth or lips are to be sealed, for a "mystery" is something on which silence must be kept. While the Greeks used the word for the everyday intimacies of life, it seems certain that its original thrust was religious and that this religious connotation was never wholly lost.

Of particular interest is a religious development in ancient Greece. From the seventh century BC to the fourth century AD a new form of worship became popular—the "mysteries." The devotees of the "mysteries" were commanded to silence, so our knowledge is fragmentary. We can, however, grasp their four leading features.

Preeminently, the "mysteries" offered an experience of *personal* communion with deity. No matter which "mystery" was involved—Eleusinian, Dionysian, the Great Mother, or Mithraism, to name but some—the worshiper at the climax of its rites would sense in an unmediated manner the presence of the god. In some, in fact, he would become identified with the deity.

Second, all the mysteries involved *cultic rites*. These sacred actions, performed before the circle of devotees, portrayed the destinies of the god. At times they were wild and irrational, as the Dionysian cult, where women butchered goats and drank their blood out on the mountains. At times they were more subdued, although still dramatic and colorful. By means of these rites the devotees entered into the fate of the god.

A third feature was *initiation*. Those who wished to enter into the celebration must first be separated—the uninitiated were denied both access to the rites and knowledge of them. Initiation came by way of offerings, purifications, vigils, and beholding secret sights. So the "mysteries" led to societies of the initiated, those who knew one another by confessional formulas and secret signs.

Finally, the "mysteries" gave hope of *eternal* life to their followers. Each of the gods was connected with the cycle of the seasons—winter with death, spring with resurrection. The gods themselves suffered, died, and were reborn each year. Similarly the initiate, by becoming united with the god, could enter the cycle of cosmic life. As he shared in the destiny of the god, the devotee acquired a share in the divine power of life.

We have described the "mysteries" because of their importance to our understanding of the rise and spread of Christianity. They show us the intensity of common man's longing to enter into a personal religious experience— a longing that time can never allay! And they give us a glimpse of that world into which Christianity was born—a world of hopes and fears, of struggle with sorrow and pain, of frailty in the face of death. They tell us, too, of the rival religions that Christianity had to combat. In important respects—the sense of personal knowledge of God and the hope of immortality—they provided sharp alternatives to our religion.

Our interest in the "mysteries" goes beyond this general background to Christianity, however. Of crucial concern to our study of Christian baptism is the relation of this rite to the "mysteries." That is, did the early Christians understand baptism as a rite of initiation that paralleled the "mystery" ceremonies? We have already seen (Chapter 3) that Paul described baptism as an entering into the death and resurrection of Jesus. Does his reasoning suggest that Christianity itself belongs to the "mystery" category? And to sharpen still further our need to investigate this matter, we have clear evidence that in the last half of the second century AD baptism was termed *mustērion*!

Let us carefully look at the New Testament evidence again. We find, first of all, that Paul used the word *mustērion* twenty-one times. Occasionally he employed it simply in the sense of "secret," as in 1 Corinthians 2:7; 13:2; 14:2. In other places, however, he used it in a strongly religious sense and in a way that showed parallels with the pagan "mysteries." For example: "To them God chose to make known how great among the Gentiles are the riches of the glory of this mystery, which is Christ in you, the hope of glory" (Colossians 1:27).

" 'For this reason a man shall leave his father and mother and be joined to his wife, and the two shall become one flesh.' This mystery is a profound one, and I am saying that it refers to Christ and the church" (Ephesians 5:31, 32).

"And also for me, that utterance may be given me in opening my mouth boldly to proclaim the mystery of the gospel" (Ephesians 6:19).

So Christianity was, in a sense, a new "mystery." It offered its followers personal fellowship with Jesus Christ, the risen Lord, in this life and the hope of endless life in His presence.

But Paul's use of *mustērion* also broke the pagan pattern. Most obviously, Christianity is *not* a secret religion. It centers in the "word of the cross" (1 Corinthians 1:18), the proclamation of the crucified and risen Jesus. The *mustērion* centers in God's eternal plan. It was kept in secret through long ages, but now it has been brought to light through the gospel (Ephesians 1:9, 10). In Christianity the "mystery" *has now been revealed!* Christianity is not a secret society of those initiated through closely guarded rites. It is a fellowship of those who have responded to the Good News of the revelation of God's mystery. So God's *mustērion* is not itself a revelation but is the object of revelation.

This New Testament use of *mustērion* shows a conscious endeavor to relate Christianity to the culture of the times—to relate and to correct. Christianity has affinity with the "mysteries," but it also stands apart from them. Paul was speaking the language of his day (as every preacher must), but only to set forth the uniqueness and challenge of the gospel in the most forceful manner.

What, then, of baptism? What connection do we find between it and the *mustērion*? The facts here are striking. Nowhere do we find baptism called a *mustērion*. Where baptism is mentioned, there is no use of *mustērion*. Where *mustērion* is mentioned, there is no clear connection with baptism. Obviously New Testament writers carefully avoided describing baptism as an initiation in parallel with the pagan "mysteries."

It is likely, however, that some of the early Christians thought of baptism in this way. Especially those who had come out of a pagan background would find such an idea attractive. Perhaps at Corinth this problem had surfaced. We notice, for instance, how Paul downgraded his own baptismal practice as he wrote to the believers there: "It has been reported to me by Chloe's people that there is quarreling among you, my brethren. What I mean is that each one of you says, 'I belong to Paul,' or 'I belong to Apollos,' or 'I belong to Cephas,' or 'I belong to Christ.' Is Christ divided? Was Paul crucified for you? Or were you baptized in the name of Paul? I am thankful that I baptized none of you except Crispus and Gaius; lest any one should say that you were baptized in my name. (I did baptize also the household of Stephanas. Beyond that, I do not know whether I baptized any one else.) For Christ did not send me to baptize but to preach the gospel, and not with eloquent wisdom, lest the cross of Christ be emptied of its power" (1 Corinthians 1:11-17).

Why was Paul glad that he had not baptized more of the Corinthians? Possibly because some of the Corinthians were thinking along the lines of the pagan mysteries, in which the devotees who underwent the rites of initiation were bound by sacred bonds to the priests who directed them in the rites. Such a misunderstanding may have led, at least in part, to the problem of factions clustered around Christian leaders. Paul, of course, would have none of such ideas: Baptism is into Christ, not into a special connection with any apostle or church leader.

The New Testament, therefore, carefully avoids equating baptism with *mustērion*. But the picture changed in the second century, when the pagan use of the term for cultic rites gained acceptance in the church. Now baptism and the Lord's Supper were called *mustēria*. At first, comparisons were made between the pagan rites and the Christian ordinances, with the former being set forth as devilish imitations of the latter. But the same basic ideas were seen in both religions, although the content differed. In both there was repetition and representation of the god's sacred actions. Along with this development of thought, a host of terms used in the "mysteries" entered Christianity.

In the late second century another word came into prominence, the Latin term *sacramentum*. The Christian writings of the first century and most of the second were in Greek. But Latin works began to appear toward the close of the second century, and eventually they superseded the Greek. *Sacramentum* was widely used and had a spectrum of meanings. One of these held significance for Christian developments—it was used for the soldier's oath. This oath was a solemn rite, in itself an act of initiation.

As the language of the church changed from Greek to Latin, the door opened for a notable expansion in the meaning of *sacramentum*. Now *sacramentum* became the usual word for *mustērion*, and it was so translated in the Latin Bible. In Christian thought the terms became full equivalents—a development far beyond the Roman usage for military oaths.

So we arrive at the sacramentalism that characterized the medieval church and that still marks the Roman Catholic Church.

Baptism as Symbol

Our study so far has pointed out the errors in a sacramental view of baptism. The Biblical rite is not magical. There is no special power in the water. The rite in and of itself cannot confer its own unique grace. So Protestants have a firm Biblical base in their rejection of Roman Catholic sacramentalism.

Yet we run the risk of falling into error at the other pole—the error of downgrading the significance of baptism. Our very denial of the sacramental view may lead us to swing the pendulum to the other extreme. And to downplay baptism is surely as serious as to raise it to a level far beyond the Biblical intent.

It may help us, as we try to crystallize our thinking about the rightful place of baptism, to consider the nature of symbolism. We often use the term *symbol* to describe baptism and the Lord's Supper. The former, we are apt to say, symbolizes death and resurrection; the latter, participation in the body and blood of the Lord. And very often we say, "They are only symbols."

Such language betrays our poverty of understanding of symbols. Religious symbols are not mere teaching devices or halfway houses on the road to reality. They are not visual aids that take us so far and then must be tossed aside because we understand the truth in itself. Far from it! Religious symbols are *indispensable*. They communicate in a way that is altogether irreplaceable. To cast off symbols is to divorce ourselves from the reality with which they are connected.

Consider our common ways of communicating with each other. Speech, of course, is preeminent. But there are other ways—a glance, a touch, a shared experience, even silence. Indeed, some nonverbal media touch us with deep emotion. Music stirs the deepest recesses of the soul. Art may move us to tears.

So with the religious life. Protestantism broke with the icons and ritualistic worship of the medieval church and instead emphasized the word—the word preached, read, sung. And there was a renewal of worship. The pulpit moved to center stage, and the congregations sang to the Lord. But we know that communication with God can be nonverbal as well. We know the truth of the admonition: "Be still, and know that I am God" (Psalm 46:10). And we have to confess that our concern with words may be used to drown out the voice of God, who speaks in the stillness.

Protestants retain but two ordinances—baptism and the Lord's Supper. (Adventists include the foot-washing service under the latter.) As we reflect upon them we realize that they have a peculiar characteristic in common. In a manner that separates them from the other elements of Christian worship, they involve a doing. With prayer, Scripture, hymn, and sermon, the *word* is foremost—the word heard, read, sung, spoken, intellectualized. But baptism and the Lord's Supper are *enacted*. The first is a physical activity that leaves no part of the body untouched.

The second centers in an act of mutual washing, eating, and drinking. Each involves the *whole* person in religious activity in an utterly irreplaceable manner.

So they are not "just" symbols. They *are* symbols, with all the richness and indispensability that the term connotes. A public testimony in favor of Jesus as Christ and Lord, no matter how eloquent or sincere, cannot take the place of baptism, even as a brilliant sermon on the meaning of the cross cannot substitute for the Lord's Supper. Only by the doing can we enter into the full reality of the truths that these symbols convey. And let us be quite sure, those truths are accessible *only* through these symbols. If we discard the symbols, we fall short of the reality with which they are bound up.

Do these ideas seem "mystical"? The experiences of life in the world help us grasp them more clearly. Consider a man and a woman in love. What will happen to their relationship if it never goes beyond mere verbal expression? "I love you," no matter how often spoken or written, is not enough. Corresponding deeds must accompany the words lest love eventually become dry and bitter.

Even so must our worship transcend verbal communication. By baptism, a single act, we commit ourselves wholly and unreservedly to Jesus Christ as Saviour and Lord. By the Lord's Supper we enter again and again into His experience of the cross.

Is it possible that there is more to baptism than we usually think? Have we downgraded this rite in our thinking? Are we so anxious to avoid the medieval error that we do not *expect* and therefore do not receive the peculiar blessing the Lord has for us in it? Has the secular pressure of our times so affected us that we have come to look upon baptism in a mechanical fashion, almost oblivious to its sacred dimension?

I do not suggest that we ought to look for a dramatic

manifestation of divine power at baptism. We are not to presume upon the activity of God. But let us not forget that Jesus taught us to baptize in the name of the Triune God— Father, Son, and Holy Spirit. And let us ever remember the original Christian baptism, when the Divine Three were manifested at the Jordan. That is the point: The Trinity is invoked and is present at a believer's baptism. A blessing is sure. Just what form it may assume is not for us to dictate.

And then there is the factor of union with the body of Christ, effected by the Spirit at baptism. That is, the baptismal rite should deeply move both old believers and the new one. The Lord is present in a marked way, and deep bonds of love and community generated by the Spirit fuse believers to one another.

C. S. Lewis, perhaps, has captured something of the essence of this sense of Christian unity. "In each of my friends there is something that only some other friend can fully bring out. By myself I am not large enough to call the whole man into activity; I want other lights than my own to show all his facets. . . . Hence true Friendship is the least jealous of loves. Two friends delight to be joined by a third, and three by a fourth, if only the newcomer is qualified to become a real friend. They can then say, as the blessed souls say in Dante, 'Here comes one who will augment our loves.' For in this love 'to divide is not to take away.' Of course the scarcity of kindred souls—not to mention practical considerations about the size of rooms and the audibility of voices—set limits to the enlargement of the circle; but within those limits we possess each friend not less but more as the number of those with whom we share him increases. In this, Friendship exhibits a glorious 'nearness by resemblance' to Heaven itself where the very multitude of the blessed (which no man can number) increases the fruition which each has of God. For every soul, seeing Him in her own way, doubtless communicates that unique vision to all the rest. That, says an old author, is why the Seraphim in Isaiah's vision are crying 'Holy, Holy, Holy' *to one another* (Isaiah vi, 3). The more we thus share the Heavenly Bread between us, the more we shall all have" (*The Four Loves* [paperback], pp. 58, 59).

So baptism *is* something special. The day of a baptism *is* a high day, for the threefold God draws near with unusual power. Therefore we *may* direct candidates to expect a unique blessing—not necessarily in a dramatic manifestation of the Spirit, but through the unseen presence of Father, Son, and Holy Spirit. Although baptism is not a sacrament in the way the medieval church understood it, it is nonetheless a symbol charged with rich and irreplaceable meaning.

7

Baptism and Our Day

Our investigation into the meaning of Biblical baptism has now run its full course. The concluding remarks of this chapter will be brief and reflective.

Christian Baptism and the World's Religions

In the opening chapter we noticed mankind's universal quest for cleansing. Over and over, no matter what the culture or the period in history, mankind has felt defiled, dirty, polluted. He has sought to be made clean, to be washed, to be purified.

And his efforts to be made clean have taken a host of forms. Some of them are quaint. Some may seem foolish or infantile. Over and over he has sought religious release from the weight of pollution. However, it has been an uneven war. Despite temporary satisfaction through pilgrimage, washings, or other rituals, defilement has returned. Religious life oscillates between periods of defilement and purification.

Christian baptism becomes more meaningful against this background, for it addresses these universal fears and hopes of mankind. As we have seen, it has strongly negative and strongly positive elements. On the one hand it points to man's *utter need*. He is a sinner, defiled before a holy God, and quite helpless to cleanse himself. So we saw the elements of repentance and confession and especially the symbolism of death and burial. On the other hand, however, it points to *glorious possibility*. Mankind can share in resurrection with Christ, in rebirth, in new life, in the joy of the Spirit's presence, in identification with Jesus in the words of approval: "Thou art my beloved Son," and in acceptance into the communion of the body of Christ.

The agent of cleansing is significant. Whereas hosts of mankind have sought, and still seek, purification through the medium of water, the water of Christian baptism is not in itself a purifying agent. For Christians, the water is wholly symbolic. The *real* agent is the invisible blood of Christ. Immersion in the water identifies the candidate with the Passion of his Lord, where alone is found cleansing from sin.

So baptism is much more than the moment of purification. Christian baptism breaks the religious pattern of mankind's defilement and purgation. No longer is there an oscillation, with defilement inevitably returning to wreak its havoc. Christian baptism is a dedication and consecration as well as a cleansing. It is the door to new life. So it is not to be repeated over and over. It signals a point in time—a point of *death* and a point of *birth*. And with this it breaks completely with the purification rituals of the world's religions.

The ordinance of foot washing, practiced by Seventh-day Adventists and a few other Christian bodies, must be understood in light of the above. Very clearly we are not to conceive of it as a minibaptism in any sense of a renewal or a repetition of baptism. Its thrust, emerging from the words and example of Jesus in John 13, is to show the meaning of Christian love, humility, and service as a preparation for the fellowship of the Lord's Supper.

As we look at Christian baptism against the backdrop of

mankind's religious aspirations, then, we see the uniqueness of the Christian claim. Against a host of rites and
ceremonies to work cleansing, Christianity proclaims but
one—one that renders null and void all others. Against a
variety of cleansing agents, Christianity sets forth but
one—one that suffices for all time and for all peoples. And
more: Christianity proclaims that this simple rite and this
agent are the only ones in which the universal need for
purification from defilement can be truly answered.

Viewed from the perspective of the total religious
thought of mankind, that is a staggering claim. In the cli-
mate of our times it may appear narrow, even intolerant.
But it is the Biblical perspective. And the experience of
men and women from every part of the world and born
amid the host of non-Christian systems testifies to its truth.

Practical Considerations

At least three practical matters emerge from the study
we have made.

First, the issue of rebaptism. There is an instance of
rebaptism in the Bible—but only one. There is counsel in
the Ellen G. White writings that permits rebaptism—but it
is scant. I fear that in these times we are turning the excep-
tion into the rule. Rebaptism, unless we are careful, may
ultimately weaken the significance of baptism in the minds
of believers. We run the risk of losing the sense of the
distinctiveness, the uniqueness, of baptism. Christian baptism is a decisive rite and is not to be repeated. Let us
beware of prostituting baptism into a pragmatic ceremony
that is used to handle difficult cases of readmission to
church fellowship. Occasional cases of rebaptism may be
justified, but they should be rare. Perhaps pastors need to
better instruct believers in the way God deals with their sin.
After Peter's fall he was not rebaptized!

Second, the baptism of children. We have touched on this matter in an earlier chapter, but it is worth mentioning again. Clearly, infant baptism is impossible on a Biblical basis. The candidate must repent, confess, and have faith in Christ. Nor should we hurry children into baptism. They should not be baptized simply because it's the thing to do along with their classmates or because of undue influence from parents, pastor, or teacher. They need to be carefully instructed, not merely doctrinally but spiritually, so that they enter baptism intelligently.

On the other hand we should avoid the opposite error of discouraging children from being baptized. There is a law of spiritual maturation in operation here. Young minds are deeply impressionable in spiritual things. When the time is ripe for baptism—definitely an individual matter—it should not be delayed. Spiritual counselors need heavenly guidance and a deep personal experience with the Lord if they are to rightly guide young minds in these years of decision.

Finally, the baptismal ceremony itself. While we would have no part in a sacramental view of baptism, we think more attention needs to be given to the actual service. We need to bring out for candidates, church members, and uncommitted onlookers the beauty and deep significance of this rite. We are usually altogether too rushed. Even when we meet to worship God on Sabbath, our minds react sharply to the approach of the noon hour. So we are apt to hurry—at least mentally—the ordinances that the Lord has given us. The Lord's Supper, coming sometimes as late as 12:15 or 12:30 PM, finds believers with minds too much on the clock. And baptism is typically sandwiched between the prayer and the offering.

A five- or ten-minute service—is this the Lord's will for the baptismal rite? We need to take a hard look at our practice, reflecting on what the Bible tells of its meaning.

We cannot avoid the question: Just as on Communion Day the Supper itself is central (the sermon being abbreviated appropriately), on a baptism day should not the rite itself be the climax of the service? Perhaps we should consider having a special service on Sabbath afternoon or evening if the 11:00 AM hour cannot be accommodated. But whether the baptism takes place in morning or afternoon, careful planning and preparation should be made so that the full meaning and appeal of this symbol may emerge.

Baptism is our commission. Baptism is our witness. Baptism is our door to life. May we learn again its deep meaning for the men and women of our day.

"And Jesus came and said to them, 'All authority in heaven and on earth has been given to me. Go therefore and make disciples of all nations, baptizing them in the name of the Father and of the Son and of the Holy Spirit, teaching them to observe all that I have commanded you; and lo, I am with you always, to the close of the age' " (Matthew 28:18-20).

"Now when they heard this they were cut to the heart, and said to Peter and the rest of the apostles, 'Brethren, what shall we do?' And Peter said to them, 'Repent, and be baptized every one of you in the name of Jesus Christ for the forgiveness of your sins; and you shall receive the gift of the Holy Spirit. For the promise is to you and to your children and to all that are far off, every one whom the Lord our God calls to him' " (Acts 2:37-39).

"What shall we say then? Are we to continue in sin that grace may abound? By no means! How can we who died to sin still live in it? Do you not know that all of us who have been baptized into Christ Jesus were baptized into his death? We were buried therefore with him by baptism into death, so that as Christ was raised from the dead by the glory of the Father, we too might walk in newness of life" (Romans 6:1-4).

"Then Jesus came from Galilee to the Jordan to John, to be baptized by him. John would have prevented him, saying, 'I need to be baptized by you, and do you come to me?' But Jesus answered him, 'Let it be so now; for thus it is fitting for us to fulfil all righteousness.' Then he consented. And when Jesus was baptized, he went up immediately from the water, and behold, the heavens were opened and he saw the Spirit of God descending like a dove, and alighting on him; and lo, a voice from heaven, saying, 'This is my beloved Son, with whom I am well pleased' " (Matthew 3:13-17).

Ellen G. White Statements About Baptism

In keeping with our Protestant heritage we have sought to establish the ideas of *Clean!* from the Bible alone. The writings of Ellen G. White, however, make many references to baptism, and they deserve careful attention. While there is no extensive treatment in any one place of the significance of baptism, they contain many helpful and beautiful statements on the topic. As an invitation to the reader for further study, we have gathered below some of the leading references.

1. The necessity of baptism: No matter how faultless one's life, baptism is needed:

"Christ has made baptism the sign of entrance to His spiritual kingdom. He has made this a positive condition with which all must comply who wish to be acknowledged as under the authority of the Father, the Son, and the Holy Spirit. Before man can find a home in the church, before passing the threshold of God's spiritual kingdom, he is to receive the impress of the divine name 'The Lord our Righteousness.' Jeremiah 23:6" (*Testimonies for the Church*, Vol. 6, p. 91).

"To these youth I am authorized to say: Repent ye and be converted, that your sins may be blotted out. There is no time for you to waste. Heaven and immortal life are valuable treasures that cannot be obtained without an effort on your part. No matter how faultless may have been your lives, as sinners you have steps to take. You are required to repent, believe, and be baptized. Christ was wholly righteous; yet He, the Saviour of the world, gave man an example by Himself taking the steps which He requires the sinner to take to become a child of God, and heir of heaven.

"If Christ, the spotless and pure Redeemer of man, condescended to take the steps necessary for the sinner to take in conversion, why should any, with the light of truth shining upon their pathway, hesitate to submit their hearts to God, and in humility confess that they are sinners, and show their faith in the atonement of Christ by words and actions, identifying themselves with those who profess to be His followers? There will ever be some who do not live out their profession, whose daily lives show them to be anything but Christians; but should this be a sufficient reason for any to refuse to put on Christ by baptism into the faith of His death and resurrection?" (*ibid.*, Vol. 4, pp. 40, 41).

"Christ made baptism the entrance to His spiritual kingdom. He made this a positive condition with which all must comply who wish to be acknowledged as under the authority of the Father, the Son, and the Holy Ghost. Those who receive the ordinance of baptism thereby make a public declaration that they have renounced the world, and have become members of the royal family, children of the heavenly King" (*SDA Bible Commentary*, Vol. 6, p. 1075).

2. Baptism signifies repentance:

"John the Baptist came preaching truth, and by his preaching sinners were convicted and converted. These would go into the kingdom of heaven before the ones who in self-righteousness resisted the solemn warning. The publicans and harlots were ignorant, but these learned men knew the way of truth. Yet they refused to walk in the path which leads to the Paradise of God. The truth that should have been to them a savor of life unto life became a savor of death unto death. Open sinners who loathed themselves had received baptism at the hands of John; but these teachers were hypocrites" (*Christ's Object Lessons*, p. 277).

"In the spirit and with the power of Elijah, John denounced the corruptions of the Jews, and raised his voice in reproving their prevailing sins. His discourses were plain, pointed, and convincing. Many were brought to repentance of their sins, and, as evidence of their repentance, were baptized of him in Jordan" (*SDA Bible Commentary*, Vol. 5, p. 1089).

3. Baptism signifies renunciation of the world:

"In baptism we are given to the Lord as a vessel to be used. Baptism is a most solemn renunciation of the world. Self is by profession dead to a life of sin. The waters cover the candidate, and in the presence of the whole heavenly universe the mutual pledge is made. In the name of the Father, the Son, and the Holy Spirit, man is laid in his watery grave, buried with Christ in baptism, and raised from the water to live the new life of loyalty to God. The three great powers in heaven are witnesses; they are invisible but present" (*ibid.*, Vol. 6, p. 1074).

"Baptism is a most solemn renunciation of the world. Those who are baptized in the threefold name of the Father, the Son, and the Holy Spirit, at the very entrance of their Christian life declare publicly that they have forsaken the service of Satan and have become members of the royal family, children of the heavenly King. They have obeyed the command: 'Come out from among them, and be ye separate, . . . and touch not the unclean thing.' And to them is fulfilled the promise: 'I will receive you, and will be a Father unto you, and ye shall be My sons and daughters, saith the Lord Almighty.' 2 Corinthians 6:17, 18" (*Testimonies*, Vol. 6, p. 91).

4. Baptism is a covenant:

"Those who . . . [receive the ordinance of baptism] are to make all worldly considerations secondary to their new relations. Publicly they have declared that they will no longer live in pride and self-indulgence. Christ enjoins those who receive this ordinance to remember that they are bound by a solemn covenant to live to the Lord. They are to use for Him all their entrusted capabilities, never losing the realization that they bear God's sign of obedience to the Sabbath of the fourth commandment, that they are subjects of Christ's kingdom, partakers of the divine nature. They are to surrender all they have and are to God, employing all their gifts to His name's glory" (*SDA Bible Commentary*, Vol. 6, p. 1075).

"The Father, the Son, and the Holy Ghost, powers infinite and omniscient, receive those who truly enter into covenant relation with God. They are present at every baptism, to receive the candidates who have renounced the world and have received Christ into the soul temple. These candidates have entered into the family of God, and their names are inscribed in the Lamb's book of life" (Ms27½, 1900; see *SDA Bible Commentary*, Vol. 6, p. 1075).

"After the believing soul has received the ordinance of baptism, he is to bear in mind that he is dedicated to God, to Christ, and to the Holy Spirit" (*Evangelism*, p. 315).

5. Baptism commemorates Christ's death, burial, and resurrection:

"And the repentant believer, who takes the steps required in conversion, commemorates in his baptism the death, burial, and resurrection of Christ. He goes down into the water in the likeness of Christ's death and burial, and he is raised out of the water in the likeness of His resurrection—not to take up the old life of sin, but to live a new life in Christ Jesus" (3SP 204; see *SDA Bible Commentary*, Vol. 5, p. 1113).

"The resurrection of Christ is commemorated by our being buried with Him by baptism, and raised out of the watery grave, in likeness of His resurrection, to live in newness of life" (*Early Writings*, p. 217).

6. Baptism is the door to new life in Christ:

"The obligations in the spiritual agreement entered into at baptism are mutual. As human beings act their part with whole-hearted obedience, they have a right to pray, 'Let it be known, Lord, that Thou art God in Israel.' The fact that you have been baptized in the name of the Father, the Son, and the Holy Spirit, is an assurance that if you will claim their help, these powers will help you in every emergency. The Lord will hear and answer the prayers of His sincere followers who wear Christ's yoke and learn in His school His meekness and lowliness" (*Evangelism* pp. 316, 317).

"The vows which we take upon ourselves in baptism embrace much. In the name of the Father, the Son, and the Holy Spirit we are buried in the likeness of Christ's death and raised in the likeness of His resurrection, and we are to live a new life. Our life is to be bound up with the life of Christ. Henceforth the believer is to bear in mind that he is dedicated to God, to Christ, and to the Holy Spirit. He is to make all worldly considerations secondary to this new relation. Publicly he has declared that he will no longer live in pride and self-indulgence. He is no longer to live a careless, indifferent life. He has made a covenant with God. He has died to the world. He is to live to the Lord, to use for Him all his entrusted capabilities, never losing the realization that he bears God's signature, that he is a subject of Christ's kingdom, a partaker of the divine nature. He is to surrender to God all that he is and all that he has, employing all his gifts to His name's glory" (*Testimonies,* Vol. 6, pp. 98, 99).

7. Baptism is the portal to the church:

"Present truth leads onward and upward, gathering in the needy, the oppressed, the suffering, the destitute. All that will come are to be brought into the fold. In their lives there is to take place a reformation that will constitute them members of the royal family, children of the heavenly King. By hearing the message of truth, men and women are led to accept the Sabbath and to unite with the church by baptism" (*ibid.*, Vol. 8, pp. 195, 196).

8. The blessings of baptism:

"The ordinances of baptism and the Lord's Supper are two monumental pillars; one without and one within the church. Upon these ordinances Christ has inscribed the name of the true God" (*ibid.*, Vol. 6, p. 91).

"As Christians submit to the solemn rite of baptism, He registers the vow that they make to be true to Him. This vow is their oath of allegiance. They are baptized in the name of the Father and the Son and the Holy Spirit. Thus they are united with the three great powers of heaven" (*Evangelism*, p. 307).

"What does this scene mean to us? How thoughtlessly we have read the account of the baptism of our Lord, not realizing that its significance was of the greatest importance to us, and that Christ was accepted of the Father in man's behalf. As Jesus bowed on the banks of Jordan and offered up His petition, humanity was presented to the Father by Him who had clothed His divinity with humanity. Jesus offered Himself to the Father in man's behalf, that those who had been separated from God through sin, might be brought back to God through the merits of the divine Petitioner. Because of sin the earth had been cut off from heaven, but with His human arm Christ encircles the fallen race, and with His divine arm He grasps the throne of the Infinite, and earth is brought into favor with heaven, and man into communion with his God. The prayer of Christ in behalf of lost humanity cleaved its way through every shadow that Satan had cast between man and God, and left a clear channel of communication to the very throne of glory. The gates were left ajar, the heavens were opened, and the Spirit of God, in the form of a dove, encircled the head of Christ, and the voice of God was heard saying, 'This is my beloved Son, in whom I am well pleased' " (*SDA Bible Commentary*, p. 1078).

"In our behalf the Saviour laid hold of the power of Omnipotence, and as we pray to God, we may know that Christ's prayer has ascended before, and that God has heard and answered it. With all our sins and weaknesses we are not cast aside as worthless. 'He hath made us accepted in the beloved.' The glory that rested upon Christ is a pledge of the love of God for us. It tells of the power of prayer—how the human voice may reach the ear of God, and our petitions find acceptance in the courts of heaven. The light that fell from the open portals upon the head of our Saviour, will fall upon us as we pray for help to resist temptation. The voice that spoke to Jesus says to every believing soul, 'This is my beloved child, in whom I am well pleased.'

"Through the gates ajar there streamed bright beams of glory from the throne of Jehovah, and this light shines even upon us. The assurance given to Christ is assurance to every repenting, believing, obedient child of God that he is accepted in the Beloved.

"Christ's prayer on the banks of the Jordan includes every one who will believe in Him. The promise that you are accepted in the Beloved comes to you. God said, 'This is my beloved Son, in whom I am well pleased.' This means that through the dark shadow which Satan has thrown athwart your pathway Christ has cleaved the way for you to the throne of the infinite God. He has laid hold of almighty power, and you are accepted in the Beloved" (ibid., p. 1079).